GREAT
SEX
GUIDE

ANNE HOOPER

GREAT
SEX
GUIDE

ANNE HOOPER

DORLING KINDERSLEY
London • New York • Sydney • Moscow
www.dk.com

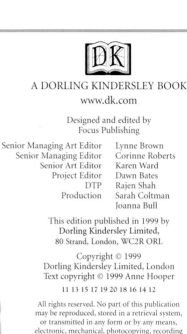

DK

A DORLING KINDERSLEY BOOK
www.dk.com

Designed and edited by
Focus Publishing

Senior Managing Art Editor	Lynne Brown
Senior Managing Editor	Corinne Roberts
Senior Art Editor	Karen Ward
Project Editor	Dawn Bates
DTP	Rajen Shah
Production	Sarah Coltman
	Joanna Bull

This edition published in 1999 by
Dorling Kindersley Limited,
80 Strand, London, WC2R ORL

A CIP catalogue record for this book is available
from the British Library.

ISBN 0–7513–0704–1

Reproduced by GRB Editrice Srl. Italy
Printed in Singapore by Star Standard

CONTENTS

FUN FLICKER ACTION

For an added turn-on, look at the top of each right-
hand page as you flick through the book and you'll
see a couple enjoying step-by-step sexual pleasure!

INTRODUCTION

THIS IS A GUIDE TO GREAT SEX. But what is "great" sex? Primarily, it is *love*making. That is, a superlative intimate interaction between you and your partner in which you can express your innermost feelings without fear, in a totally relaxed and comfortable frame of mind. It is about intense physical sensation, but it also involves a cathartic process of spiritual discovery and fulfillment.

RELEASING YOUR SEXUAL ENERGY

Above all, great lovemaking is a process of sharing sexual and emotional energy at their most highly charged, with the one you love.

Everyone deserves great sex, and everyone can share it, with a loving and understanding partner and a little help. This book is designed to provide that help. In it you will find something that I can suggest but that only you and your

LOVE TO BE LOVED
Learn to take time over lovemaking, reveling in the gradual release of your sexual energy, and the experience can become wonderful once more.

partner can put into action – the activity of tapping into your sexual energy. And sexual energy is a version of the body's "natural electricity" – the invisible force-field of power that is within and which surrounds us all, every day of our lives.

ENERGIZING ONE ANOTHER
You can help your partner to discover their sexual energy by tapping into your own.

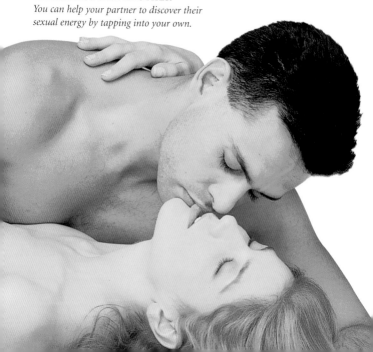

The idea that the body possesses energy was conceived in ancient times. The ancient Chinese believed that certain meridian points on the body, if correctly stimulated, charged the individual with energy.

To reach these hidden power points, you begin by throwing away the idea that spontaneity is the only good way in which to experience lovemaking. The ancient *Tao of Sex* described some very specific actions to be practiced as a kind of discipline with the ultimate aim of arousing energy. Spontaneous lovemaking is wonderful but so are lots of other methods of merging body and soul – and, in the process, enjoying truly great sex.

REKINDLING THE MAGIC

Do you remember the early occasions on which you and your partner made love – when things were going well, when you felt relaxed and natural together, and lovemaking was such joy and fun that you tumbled about in bed like puppies? Do you remember stretching out with the pure luxury of all that sensuality? Those were wonderful days when you discovered sensuality for the first time. You can't, of course, recreate a first time, but with this book you can learn how to recharge your sexual batteries, rediscover the joy of making love with your partner and the enlightenment of spiritual discovery and fulfillment, through the greatest sexual experiences you can imagine.

Anne J. Hooper

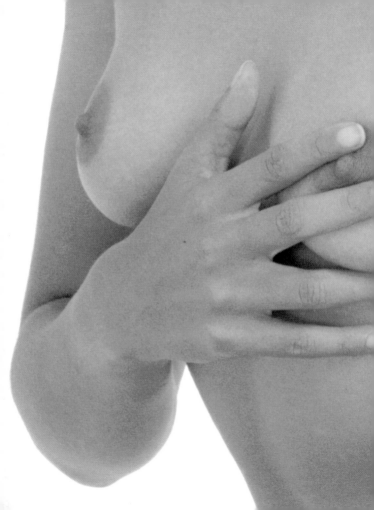

FREEING YOUR SEXUAL ENERGY

Investing a little time in preparing your mind
and body for the pleasures to come will reap
wonderful rewards. What if you could discover
ways of focusing single-mindedly on sexual
pleasure and losing all inhibitions about your
body? What if you could find ways of tapping
into your innermost spiritual and bodily energy,
of elevating your lovemaking to a higher plain?
Read on, and learn how.

RELAXATION AND ENERGY

MOST OF THE ACTIVITIES described in this book are designed for two people to carry out together. This is because, for the majority of people at least, the most pleasurable way to expand and expend sexual energy is in the company of a lover. However, the exercises described in this opening section differ slightly in that they pave the way for the build-up of sexual energy in the individual's body. Of course, you are free to carry out the exercises in each other's company, if you prefer.

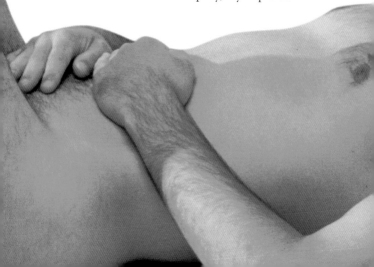

PREPARE TO RELAX

It is not always easy simply to "switch off." Relaxation takes preparation: loose clothing – or none at all – a comfortable place to lie down, and total, undisrupted privacy.

Close your eyes to enjoy deep relaxation

TENSION VERSUS RELAXATION

Not all relaxation is desirable – if you relaxed to the point of being comatose, life would shudder to a halt. Sexual energy is no exception to this rule. When your body is exceptionally physically relaxed, its inclination is to go to sleep rather than be fired up with sexual enthusiasm. However, when you embrace that rare and invigorating state of being mentally relaxed but physically alert, you achieve a type of sexual balance that can lead to wonderfully satisfying feelings. Paradoxically, one way of arriving at such a state is by starting off relaxed in both body *and* mind.

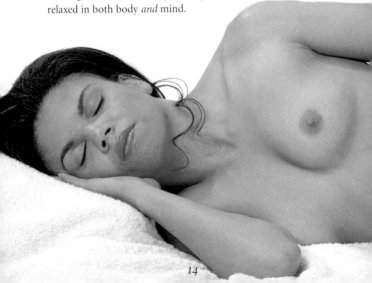

DELIBERATE STRESS

We achieve bodily relaxation best by deliberately putting the body under stress then feeling how relaxed it can become in contrast. Most people think that in order to experience orgasm you need to be relaxed. Yet orgasm itself is composed of a mixture of relaxed mental state and tensed muscular activity. So consider relaxation as a starting point for several different aspects of sexuality.

Stroke yourself to help relax and release tension

LEARNING TO RELAX

With practice, after a while you will find it easier to relax. Close your eyes, make a conscious effort to free your mind, lie still, and stroke yourself comfortingly.

HOW TO TENSE AND RELAX

STRESS AND RELAXATION are opposite sides of the same coin; without one, you cannot have the other. The exercises that follow help you to achieve complete relaxation by deliberately putting the body under stress, so you can feel how relaxed it can become in contrast. They also teach you about bodily energy – your first step in the journey toward sexual dynamism.

LYING DOWN COMFORTABLY

Place a towel on the floor and lie down flat on your back. Breathe in slowly through your nose and out through your mouth. After a couple of minutes, start noticing, while you continue with the breathing, which parts of your body feel tense.

Exhale slowly through your mouth to maximize your growing sense of relaxation

IDENTIFYING TENSION SPOTS

As you become aware of your tension spots, clench these areas hard for a count of three and then let go. If you find it difficult to identify tension spots, or if you feel tense all over, try working your way up through the whole body, first tensing, then relaxing. Begin at the tip of the right foot and work your way up the right leg. When you reach the top, go back down to the left foot and come up that leg. Once you reach the abdomen, work your way up it, all the way to the neck, tensing and relaxing as you continue.

Focus on the parts of your body that feel tense. With practice, you will be able to clench and relax every muscle

SETTING THE MOOD
Choose a quiet, comfortable place in which to lie down. The right environment is essential for deep relaxation.

17

TENSING THE FACE

The face can be exercised, too. Begin by squeezing your chin onto your neck hard, for a count of three, then relax. Then tip your head backward so that you are looking at the ceiling, hold, and let go. Tense each side of your face, hold, and relax. Open your mouth wide, hold, then let go.

TOTAL RELAXATION

Once you have tensed and relaxed every inch of your body, examine yourself for remaining spots of tension. If you find any, simply tense these areas again until you are relaxed all over.

MIND AND BODY IN HARMONY
Keep focusing on any parts of your body that remain tense.

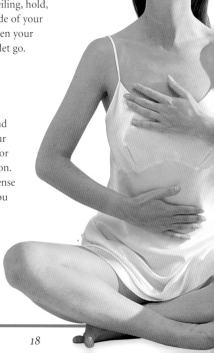

Slow Movements

Take your time when you finish relaxing. Don't immediately undo all your new-found calmness! When you sit up, don't just sit bolt upright. Wait a while, savoring the stillness of your limbs. Tell yourself that there is no hurry to rise. Roll over onto your front and come up backward and slowly. This prevents the blood from rushing from the head, making you feel faint.

Savor the moment
Once standing, raise your arms slowly above your head as you breathe deeply. Feel the energy surge within you.

The Importance of Breathing

While tensing it's easy to forget to continue breathing slowly and steadily. When we feel tense and hurried, we breathe in short, shallow gasps. Deliberately slowing down your breathing will help to aid the rest of the calming process.

BODILY ENERGY

THE IDEA THAT THE HUMAN BODY possesses a kind of invisible force field (which can be described as energy) is not a new one. If we breathe fully, we can feel energy by using deliberate bodily tension to "open" ourselves. But be prepared: some people get quite a shock when they first feel the flow of sexual energy.

Let the energy emanate from your raised palms

FEEL YOUR ENERGY
By tuning into each other's energy, you and your lover will enjoy physical and spiritual harmony.

THE VALUE OF BREATHING CORRECTLY

Breathing deeply is one of the keys to releasing emotion. Some of us get used to "not breathing," or to breathing only in short, shallow bursts. By doing this we may prevent ourselves from experiencing "bad" feelings, but we also lose out because we prevent ourselves from enjoying "good" feelings.

KIRLIAN ENERGY

Kirlian photography demonstrates that all living objects radiate a force field of energy that can be altered, depending on the subject's state of health. The bioenergetic exercises, in the following section, demonstrate how humans can improve the overall strength and quality of their bodily energy.

HOW TO BREATHE CORRECTLY

Breathe from the diaphragm. This means taking deep, slow breaths, in through the nose and out through the mouth. If you don't know whether you are doing this correctly, place your hand across the gap in the ribs just below the chest. As you breathe in, can you feel the ribs lift and expand? If all you can feel is your stomach going in and out, then you've got it wrong. Deliberately shift the activity upward. This regular breathing from the diaphragm underlies all of the exercises on the following pages.

BIOENERGY

A WHOLE SET of physical exercises has grown up out of the school of thought that is "bioenergy." These will put you more in touch with your body, release energy, and serve as a great prelude to lovemaking.

THE ENERGY FLOW

Grounding is a bioenergetic exercise that helps you to sense the energy that flows through both the ground and you. As well as being pleasurable and relaxing, the exercise will put you in touch with your inner force. Grounding is a great way of enabling you to feel the power in your body, particularly in your upper legs and pelvis.

FEEL THE VIBRATION
When you've done this exercise a couple of times, you'll feel a vibration in the tops of your legs that signals the energy flow.

GROUNDING

Push your fists into the small of your back to help concentrate the energy flow in your pelvic region

1 Stand with your feet firmly apart at a distance of about 18 in (46 cm). Point your toes in toward each other, bend your knees slightly, and press your fists into your back, just above the waist.

2 Let your head fall back and, at the same time, press your heels firmly down on the ground. Visualize the ground as a giant energy source and you as a tree or a plant, tapping into this energy. Don't let up on this heel pressure. Hold the stance for as long as your legs and neck can bear it, breathing from the diaphragm throughout.

3 Stand up straight, on the out-breath, then let the top half of your body fall forward so that your hands are nearly touching the ground. Hold this, while still grounding those heels constantly. After a couple of minutes stand up straight again and relax.

4 After carrying out the exercise a couple of times, you should start to feel a vibration in the tops of your legs. This vibration signals the release of the energy flow.

FINISH IN STYLE
When you have finished doing the grounding exercise, lie down on your bed and allow yourself to relax for a minute or two before giving your body and genitals a sensual massage. Focus your mind on the middle of your body and the tops of your legs, and contemplate the energy surge you have just experienced.

PELVIC LIFT

While some people discover their entire body
comes alive during lovemaking, others only feel a
sensation in the genitals. By doing pelvic exercises,
you will learn how to "open" your body more fully.

The first exercise is the pelvic lift: lie flat on
your back, with your knees drawn up and your
arms along your sides, palms down. Push up your
bottom and arch your back. Your feet, shoulders,
neck, and head should be the only parts of your
body touching the floor. Press your heels down,
grounding them with the earth's energy. Hold this
for a couple of minutes, then let your body down
again. You may feel vibrations in your thighs as
well as sensations in the pelvis.

*Let the energy
flow up
through your
thighs and
throughout
your pelvic
region*

WARNING
Men and women with back problems should not carry out pelvic exercises.

LOOSENING UP THE BODY

By using deep breathing and by actively encouraging the build up of pelvic tension, we can learn how to stress our bodies beneficially. Moving with ease and freeing stiff limbs is part of the process. Understanding your own individual pattern of sexual tension and climax is another.

PELVIC EXERCISES
Simple pelvic movements release sexual energy throughout the body.

PELVIC ROCK

Lie on your back, palms down and legs flat. On an in-breath, arch your back (keeping your bottom on the ground) and let your pelvis fall away from the direction of your head. On an out-breath, press your spine to the ground and pull your pelvis toward the direction of your head. By doing these two movements, you will realize you are rocking your pelvis. Repeat 10 times.

WALL EXERCISE

This is a variation of the pelvic lift, only instead of doing it on the floor, you do it with your legs up against a wall. It's very like the "walking up the wall" game small children sometimes play.

Lie with your buttocks against a wall and place the soles of your feet squarely on the wall itself. Rock your pelvis back as you breathe in, and lift your spine a little higher from the ground. With each in-breath, lift the spine another vertebra higher until you have reached as high as feels comfortable. Your body forms an arch. Then, on an out-breath, let your body relax back down.

Swing your hips smoothly and easily, around and around

PELVIC CIRCLING

Stand with your feet 18 in (46 cm) apart and move your hips in a circle, as if you were hula-dancing or hula-hooping. Move forward, side, back, side, around and around. Become aware of how you are breathing and ensure that you breathe evenly and rhythmically while you circle. It may help you to imagine a hula-hoop whirring around and around your hips. You may hoop clockwise, then counter-clockwise, then in a figure eight. The aim of the exercise is to free the pelvis of stiffness and rigidity.

PELVIC CIRCLING
This bioenergetic exercise eases the pelvis and helps you to feel the flow of energy in and around your genitals.

ENJOY YOURSELF
Dress comfortably, free your mind, and enjoy yourself when performing bioenergetic exercises. Allowing yourself this time to discover and unlock your sexual energy is liberating, builds self-confidence, and increases sexual awareness. It can take some getting used to, but it is worth the effort.

LOSING INHIBITIONS

HANG-UPS PREVENT US from being fulfilled. The impact of childhood commands – "thou shall not touch thyself," "thou shall avoid appearing ridiculous at all costs" – is the greatest culprit. The following exercises are designed not just to awaken pelvic sensation, but also to test and overcome childhood shame.

Our parents inherited attitudes about sexuality that were originally vested in their grandparents. The legacy for us is that we struggle with outdated mental controls that we may not even know have been lodged inside us. As children, we cannot escape our family's attitudes and examples.

LET GO, AND LIBERATE
You cannot fully release yourself until you free your mind of deep-seated prejudices about sex.

Gently caress every inch of your body

ALL FOURS

Position yourself on all fours facing away from the wall and place the soles of your feet against it. Rock your pelvis back on an in-breath (bottom up) and then forward on an out-breath. As you rock back, push with your hands against the floor. As you rock forward, push against the walls with your heels. Do this 10 times. It is only your pelvis that moves. Do not come farther forward with the rest of your body.

THINK POSITIVE

The exercises on this and the following page not only ask you to leave any preconceptions behind, they ask you deliberately to encourage what might seem like ridiculous behavior and body poses. Exaggerate the poses. Examine your feelings. Can you bear them? Can you enjoy them? Relax, and develop your sexuality.

BOTTOMS UP

On all fours, rest your head on the floor, with your arms spread out on the ground on either side of your head, and your bottom sticking up into the air. Deliberately exaggerate how far you can make your bottom jut out. As you do so, grow aware of the following sensations: expansion in the chest; a loosening and relaxation of the stomach; and a sense of the buttocks opening and spreading.

SQUATTING

This exercise is designed principally for women, as it opens up and relaxes the female genital area, although men can try it out if they wish.

Squat down, knees bent and out to the side, with your arms inside your legs and your heels on the floor. Since most of us are not contortionists, it may be advisable to begin by putting a book beneath your heels. Hold onto something if you need to keep your balance. The object is to open up and relax the genital area while maintaining rhythmical breathing.

RELAX AND ENJOY
If you feel silly doing any of these exercises, don't worry. Just stay with your feelings and get used to them. You'll soon find you enjoy the experience.

WARNING
People with knee injuries may either do this by lowering themselves slowly, first taking the weight of the body on their hands to reduce sudden knee pressure, or may leave it out altogether.

MEN ONLY

One problem males sometimes experience is feeling *too* tense in and around the genitals, which can prevent the penis and testes dropping down. The testicle pull is a method of letting the genitals relax and of defusing sexual arousal. It can be done in any position that feels comfortable.

Take a testicle in each hand and gently pull down. Hold for a count of three and then let go. Do this about 20 times, or more if genital tension is extreme.

AN ECSTATIC RELEASE

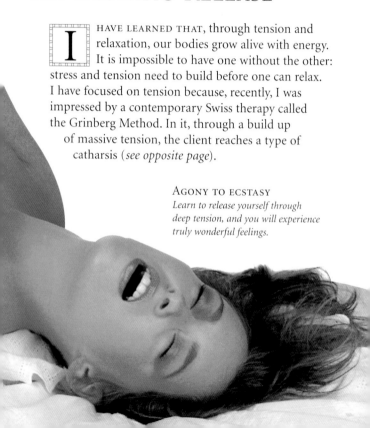

I HAVE LEARNED THAT, through tension and relaxation, our bodies grow alive with energy. It is impossible to have one without the other: stress and tension need to build before one can relax. I have focused on tension because, recently, I was impressed by a contemporary Swiss therapy called the Grinberg Method. In it, through a build up of massive tension, the client reaches a type of catharsis (*see opposite page*).

AGONY TO ECSTASY
Learn to release yourself through deep tension, and you will experience truly wonderful feelings.

BUILDING TENSION

By using the force of their entire body, the client pushes
against the therapist, breathing in whatever exaggerated
way feels right. The result is an almost orgiastic sensation
of gut emotion joined to a terrific build up of bodily tension.
In a less exaggerated form, by carrying out the bioenergetic
exercises shown on pages 22–27 I am asking you to
deliberately put your body under similar stress. You, too,
may be able to reach a state of body tension which ultimately
results in deep relaxation.

CATHARSIS

The result of the bioenergetic exercises should be a "letting go"
of such heightened tension that it's cathartic. Stress feelings
disappear. Deep shoulder pain loses layers of agony. It's
possible to end up looking as if you have just stepped out
of a bed of passion.

TRUE INTIMACY

Building and releasing tension isn't necessarily a sexual process.
But it is an intimate one. You will experience each other in a way
most of us only get close to with a lover. With bioenergetic
exercises you should reach a heightened body state that
leads naturally to lovemaking.

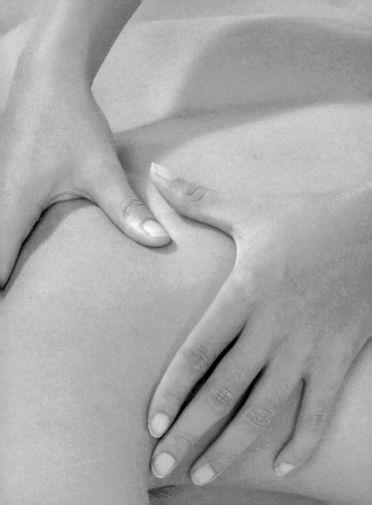

Sensual Massage

Part of the process of releasing sexual energy
is preparing the body for the counterpoints of
tension and release that will occur in any
extended session of lovemaking. Massage is
part of that preparation. There are many
wonderful massage techniques that can be
employed, some of which charge the body with
electricity, and others that soothe away stresses
and cares and prepare you for the joys to follow.

THE POWER OF TOUCH

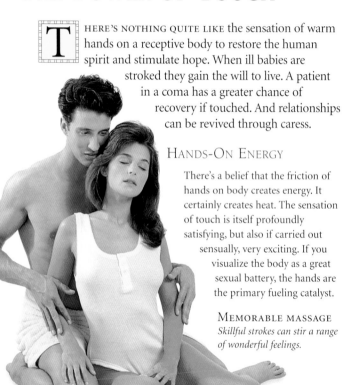

THERE'S NOTHING QUITE LIKE the sensation of warm hands on a receptive body to restore the human spirit and stimulate hope. When ill babies are stroked they gain the will to live. A patient in a coma has a greater chance of recovery if touched. And relationships can be revived through caress.

HANDS-ON ENERGY

There's a belief that the friction of hands on body creates energy. It certainly creates heat. The sensation of touch is itself profoundly satisfying, but also if carried out sensually, very exciting. If you visualize the body as a great sexual battery, the hands are the primary fueling catalyst.

MEMORABLE MASSAGE
Skillful strokes can stir a range of wonderful feelings.

GOLDEN RULES

The fingertips are capable of creating overwhelming sensation all over the body. But in order to obtain the maximum pleasure from the experience, there are certain golden rules that should always be observed.

◆ *Make sure the massage room remains consistently warm.*

◆ *Ensure that the massage oil and your hands are warmed.*

◆ *Guarantee that you have uninterrupted privacy.*

◆ *Massage on the floor (covered with towels) or on a massage table – not on a bed.*

◆ *Support the head with a low pillow.*

◆ *Ensure that the massage oil smells attractive (baby oil will not do).*

◆ *Make sure that your hands are scrupulously clean – dirt can hurt the skin.*

◆ *Pour a little of the oil into your hands and coat them before applying to your partner's skin – do not, ever, drop oil onto the body.*

◆ *Apply the oil with quick, firm strokes.*

◆ *Once you have begun the massage proper, deliberately slow down all strokes and never lose touch again until the end of the massage.*

SENSATIONAL MASSAGE

ALL OF MASSAGE IS SENSUAL. But, as George Orwell might have said, some strokes are more sensual than others. Some areas of the body spark into life quickly, while certain atmospheres definitely increase sensuality. Most of you will know about the electricity that is obtained by rubbing two pieces of silky material together, or by brushing your hair and then picking up scraps of paper by holding the hairbrush next to them. The electrical charge on the brush acts as a "magnet."

SOFTLY DOES IT
When massaging, always try to be sensitive to your partner's needs.

CHANGING THE RULES

An alternative massage consists of brushing different kinds of fabric against the skin. Choose sensual materials such as fur, feathers, or velvet and always begin the massage on a dry body surface, making sure your partner is comfortable.

Use your hands to find the most responsive areas

SEXY TEXTURES

W HEN I WAS LEARNING MASSAGE in highly alternative San Francisco in the mid-1970s, we used many aids. I remember arriving home from one trip bearing a massage glove – one side of it was red velvet, the other rabbit fur. I also invested in a red edible bikini that my lover was supposed to bite off me (actually it didn't taste very good), a foot roller, and a sort of loofah composed of large wooden beads that rolled as you rubbed them up and down your back.

MASSAGE AIDS

In our massage class we also experimented with stimulating textures such as:

◆ *silk*
◆ *satin*
◆ *velvet*
◆ *voile*
◆ *shiny pvc*
◆ *and – with those of us who had it – our own long, silky hair.*

NATURAL TEXTURES
Long and soft hair makes a wonderful natural massage aid when swept across the body.

ROUGH OR SMOOTH?

Everybody enjoys different bodily sensations. Ask your partner what she prefers.

CHANGING TEXTURES

The time to use different textures is after the body has already been subjected to some deep pressure massage so that it is relaxed and receptive. When you are using fabrics, avoid massage oil, as it clogs up the fabrics, rendering them useless.

DIFFERENT SENSATIONS

Each fabric feels subtly different to the next and my preference is to graduate them so that the harder fabrics, such as pvc, are used first and the softer, more erotic textures, such as wonderful long hair, are used last. Use these lightly and teasingly and, above all, slowly; when they work – wow! – you really know you have had a massage!

CREATING THE MOOD

IT MAY SEEM ODD THAT THE APPEARANCE of the room in which you are being massaged has an impact on your body, but it does. The old 1970s model worked – exotic Eastern drapes, drifts of patchouli and jasmine scenting the air, palm trees stacked around the room, and hours of harmonious music played on a tape. Atmosphere affects how we think of the experience, registering in the brain and affecting all our sensory perceptions so that our pleasure is enhanced.

COMFORT IS ALL

Sympathetic decor, and sensual sound, lighting, and fragrances create a receptive mood for massage, but you still need to be physically comfortable as well. Stack piles of colorful, fluffy towels around the massage site as a finishing touch.

HARMONIOUS ENVIRONMENT
Candlelight, incense, and aromatic oils help to enhance the right mood.

CREATING ATMOSPHERE

◆ *Invest in scented candles and light them all over the room. Do not use any other lighting.*

◆ *Turn the heating up high so that the room feels like a Turkish bath.*

Ensure your hands are clean, smooth, and warm before touching your partner

SENSUAL BODY SITES

MANY PARTS OF THE BODY are extremely sensitive and will respond to good, sensual massage. Never exclusively target the erotic sites. Instead, talk to your partner about what feels good, experiment with slow, tantalizing touch, and keep your massage strokes as smooth, continuous, and flowing as possible.

SENSUAL HOTSPOTS
People have different "hotspots." Ask what they are before you begin the massage.

SENSITIVE AREAS
The most sensitive areas of the body usually are:
◆ *head and neck*
◆ *ears*
◆ *sides of the body from armpits to hips*
◆ *inner thighs*
◆ *fingers and toes*
◆ *and, of course, the genitals.*

FEEL THE HEAT

FOR AN ENERGY MASSAGE to gain heat and provide pleasure, begin by focusing on your aim. Try to sense, through touch, the growth of the body's electrical charge – yours and your partner's – and then concentrate on this feeling throughout the massage.

SAVOR THE SENSATION

Close your eyes and revel in the feeling of your hands on your partner's body. See your hands as slowly sending out waves of heat. Your partner, in turn, should focus on your stroking and teasing and picture their body as slowly drawing in power.

As you relax into sensuality, imagine the gradual lighting up of a halo of power. "See" this energy in your mind's eye.

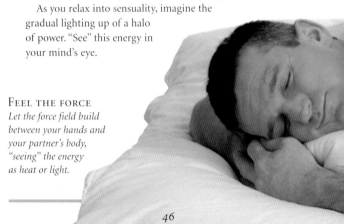

FEEL THE FORCE
Let the force field build between your hands and your partner's body, "seeing" the energy as heat or light.

46

VISUALIZE YOUR ENERGY

The energy surrounds the body in a shimmering haze. Everyone of us
contains pure energy. It pulsates through us, affecting every facet of our
lives, our emotional and physical well-being. If we are aware of this
energy in our lovemaking, we can derive more pleasure and satisfaction.

*Let your warm
breath stimulate
your partner's skin*

SENSUAL STROKES

THERE ARE MANY DIFFERENT massage strokes that have a whole range of uses, from soothing tired muscles to relieving the stresses of everyday life. Most of them also work well as a wonderful prelude or alternative to lovemaking.

TRYING DIFFERENT TECHNIQUES

Circling is still the main medium of sensual massage, but it is how you do it, and at what depth and pressure, that counts. Try:

- ◆ fingertip circling
- ◆ finger*nail* circling
- ◆ scratching
- ◆ hair sweep
- ◆ stroking with fabrics

SENSITIVE AREAS
A man's chest and nipples are often as sensitive as his partner's.

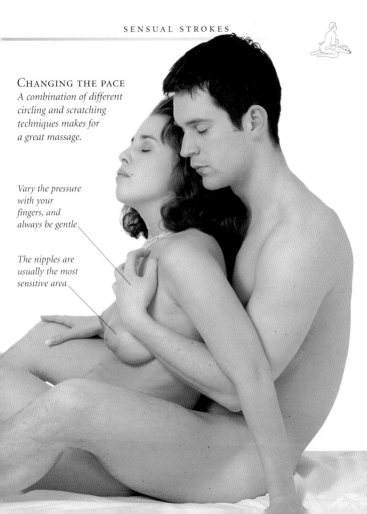

CHANGING THE PACE
A combination of different circling and scratching techniques makes for a great massage.

Vary the pressure with your fingers, and always be gentle

The nipples are usually the most sensitive area

The Impact of Pressure

Deep pressure feels healthy and reassuring; medium pressure feels pleasurable and sensual; and light pressure begins to be erotic. The key to using the many different sensual massage strokes effectively lies in delivering the right amount of physical force at the right pace. The following techniques require different degrees of pressure, but they should all be administered *slowly*.

MODULATING PRESSURE

Alternate the pressure you apply – from a stroke of your hair to a firm press of the hand – for maximum stimulation.

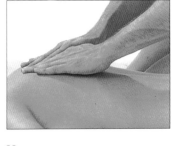

HEALING HANDS

Warm, smooth hand pressure – varied throughout the massage – will induce feelings of both eroticism and well-being.

Sweep your hair erotically over his body

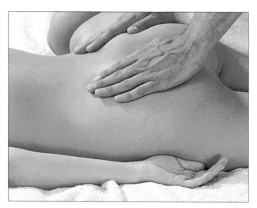

GLIDING

This is a heavy stroke because you are actually leaning on your partner. She will experience it as a sense of overwhelming ripple, like a wave that flows directly along the back.

THE GLIDE

I think this is the most spectacular movement in any massage. It's used on the back only. Place your hands on the lowest part of your partner's bottom with the palms flat and the fingers pointing toward the head. Then, with the weight of your body directed from the solar plexus, start pushing both hands up along the spine, taking as long as you like. When you reach the shoulders and neck, lightly bring your hands down again to the buttocks and recommence.

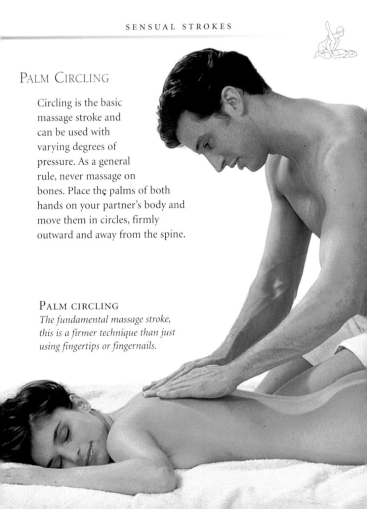

PALM CIRCLING

Circling is the basic massage stroke and can be used with varying degrees of pressure. As a general rule, never massage on bones. Place the palms of both hands on your partner's body and move them in circles, firmly outward and away from the spine.

PALM CIRCLING

The fundamental massage stroke, this is a firmer technique than just using fingertips or fingernails.

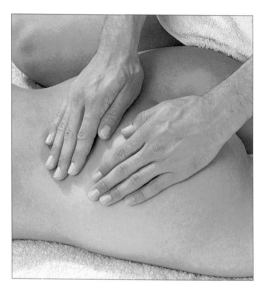

CROSS-CURRENTS
"Swimming" is also known as "cross-currents," because the technique involves moving the hands at different tempos.

SWIMMING

The hands, palm down, move in circles, close together, but in opposite directions to each other, taking on a kind of "swimming" sensation. This can be carried out up and down all the fleshy parts of the body, including the buttocks.

THUMBING

Working with both thumbs positioned on the lower back, make short, rapid, alternate strokes with each thumb, moving up and across the buttocks toward the waist. Continue up the right-hand side of the body all the way to the shoulders, repeat on the left-hand side and finish off concentrating again on the buttocks.

FIRM THUMBS
Press lightly but firmly with your thumbs, and rock the flesh beneath them rather than scraping over the surface of the skin.

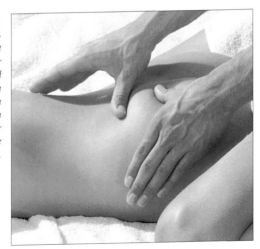

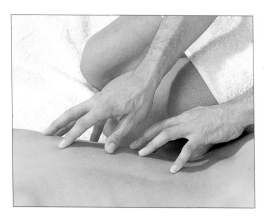

CARE WITH YOUR NAILS

If you have long fingernails, be careful not to take "clawing" too literally. You don't want to scratch and hurt your partner.

CLAWING

With only your fingertips resting on the skin, pull down firmly, hand over hand, along one side of the body and then the other. Try to keep the strokes as long and continuous as possible.

TOPPING UP

To apply more oil, keep the back of one hand resting on your partner's body, cup it, and then pour a little oil into it.

SWEEPING STROKES

When you are massaging relatively large areas of the body, such as the back, use long, sensuous, sweeping strokes. Try to keep the sensations your partner feels as continuous as possible.

SWEEPING
Be firm with your hands, and use long, continuous strokes to ensure an effective sweeping technique.

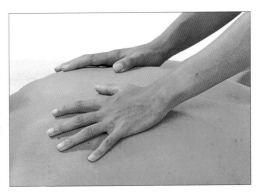

SHORT STROKES

The smaller, more complicated parts of the body such as the arms, hands, and feet, should receive short and decisive strokes. Avoid massaging areas where the bone is close to the surface of the skin.

ENERGIZING THE BACK

BEFORE THE HUMAN BODY can generate sensual energy, it needs to be freed of everyday tension. This is paradoxical, since it is by tensing the body that we come to sexual arousal and climax. But, to put it simply, it seems that there's "good" and "bad" tension.

The first back strokes therefore need to be firm, lifting the tension up and away from the spinal column. Once your partner feels relaxed, then the body begins to be receptive to the surface strokes, which are more distinctly erotic in overall sensation.

GOOD AND BAD TENSION
The stress of the day that has been carried around inside your frame, especially within the spine, counts as "bad" tension.

SPINAL RELEASE
The effect that your partner feels is of having the strain moved out of the spine and away through the sides of the body.

WEIGHTING

Sitting by your partner's side, place your hands on either side of the spine, just below the waistline. Lean heavily on your hands, applying the pressure evenly and allowing the force of your body to move your hands apart and down toward the hips as slowly as possible. They will slide apart. Move your hands down the back slightly and repeat the same movement several times, moving from the waist down to the area just above the tail of the spine.

THE GLIDE AGAIN

Repeat this stroke (*see page 52*) after doing the
Weighting stroke. The Glide is another effective
deep pressure move that shifts pressure away from
the spine and out through the top of the body.

SPINAL TAP

Press your thumbs into the indentations on either
side of your partner's spine, starting at the neck,
and draw them slowly down until you reach the
spinal base. Repeat, varying the pressure.

CORRECT PRESSURE

*Be careful not to
press the spine
itself, as pressure
on bones can be
very painful.*

SMOOTH HANDS
As you slide your thumbs up your partner's back, try to avoid contact between the rest of your hands and your partner's back.

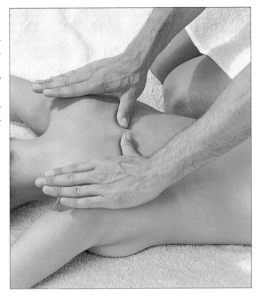

THE THUMB SLIDE

In this reverse version of the spinal tap, push your thumbs firmly up on either side of the spine, sending them from the base of the spine to the hairline. Repeat, varying the pressure.

BODY ROCKING

Kneel at your partner's right-hand side, reach across with your left hand, and slip your fingers under her body. Pull up to lift the body slightly, then release it. Slip your right hand under the same side and repeat. Pull rhythmically, each hand in turn, to set the body into a rocking pattern. Then repeat the technique on the other side of your partner's body.

WARNING
Body rocking can be difficult on a heavy person. If your partner is too large for you to lift safely, avoid this movement altogether, as you could easily strain your back.

FIRM HANDS
Handle your partner firmly yet sensitively when performing body rocking, so that she feels secure in the movement.

HIP LIFT

Glide your hands down your partner's body from the shoulders to the buttocks, then slip your hands under the hips, and draw them up the underside of the body. This will lift the body slightly. Repeat.

REPEATING STROKES

Once these pressure removal strokes have been carried out, the basic strokes can be used in a leisurely fashion, to tease the skin and lift energy levels. Feel free to improvise and to respond to your partner's indications of pleasure. Keep in mind that the slower the massage, the more impact it has.

HANDLE WITH CARE
Hold your partner firmly, and lift her slowly and gently, making sure your hands do not slip. Pinched skin is not part of a soothing massage.

Lift gently to avoid straining the back

ENDING BACK MASSAGE

AFTER 20 MINUTES OF BACK MASSAGE, your partner should be feeling pretty fired up. So it's a good idea to end with a routine that feels firm, but also clears away some of the energy generated so far.

FINISHING OFF

The object of this technique is to settle your partner and prepare her for the end of the massage. While you need to dissipate some of the energy generated during the massage as a whole, be careful not to undo all the good that has been done in the preceding 20 minutes.

1 Kneeling at your partner's side, place the backs of your forearms close together across the center of her body. Then very slowly spread your arms apart and turn them slightly inward.

2 When your arms reach the neck and buttocks, the fronts of your forearms will be in contact with your partner's shoulders and buttocks. Lift them off and repeat the stroke.

Begin the stroke with your hands palms-up

FRONT MASSAGE

MANY NEWCOMERS TO MASSAGE hesitate when faced with a partner's front. Both sexes meet with the uncertainty of how to treat the genitals. Anxiety creeps in. Fortunately, the necessity to take massage slowly means we have a chance to get more comfortable.

THE SLIDE

In back massage, circling is the basic stroke. In front massage, the slide takes its place and is the best stroke with which to begin.

Kneel at your partner's head and place your hands, palm down, on his chest, with the heels of your hands next to his armpits. Lean forward and slide your hands slowly over your partner's body until you can reach no farther; repeat two or three times. If your partner is female, reduce pressure when your fingers slip over her breasts.

RESPECT VULNERABILITY
It is imperative that your partner feels comfortable as he lies on his back.

BE GENTLE

In practical terms, massage should always be gentle. Touching breasts may only be carried out after permission has been sought and given and, for the moment, the genitals should be excluded.

Take your weight on your legs as you lean forward

HEAD MASSAGE

WHEN TENSION BUILDS in the human body, it often ends up concentrated in the shoulders, neck, and back of the head. People complaining of stress mention these feelings more than any other symptom. However, there is help at hand; a good, slow head and shoulder massage can dispel tension and induce relaxation.

HEAD AND SHOULDER LIFT

Slip your hands under your partner's shoulders, then draw them up and out, lifting the shoulders as you do so. A variation is to pull your hands along the underside of the head, with your fingers against the back of the neck.

REDUCING PRESSURE
Keeping your partner's head supported, repeatedly draw each hand in turn from the nape of the neck to the crown.

CARESSING THE HEAD

The head as a whole is an incredibly sensitive part of the human body. The scalp alone is home to countless different nerve endings, making it especially responsive to gentle massage and stroking. A head caress can be wonderfully calming.

BREAST MASSAGE

WHEN YOU ARE GIVING YOUR FEMALE PARTNER a body massage, don't be nervous about including her breasts in the routine – if you leave them out, she may be left feeling that the massage has not been properly finished. The simple but very sensual four-step breast massage routine shown overleaf was devised by the noted Californian masseur, Ray Stubbs.

TENDERLY DOES IT
Your partner's breasts are very sensitive, so make sure you always handle them gently.

HEALTHY PLEASURE
As well as being an extremely pleasurable experience for the recipient, a good breast massage stimulates nerve endings and improves blood flow.

Gently circle your partner's nipples

THE RAY STUBBS TECHNIQUE

1 Slide the flat of your left hand diagonally across your partner's left breast, moving slowly toward her right shoulder. Then slide your right hand across her right breast in the same manner. Repeat these two strokes alternately, about six or seven times each.

2 Using a well-oiled fingertip and the lightest possible touch, place your finger gently and trace out a spiral on one of your partner's breasts. Start on the outer side and spiral in smoothly and gradually until you reach the nipple, then repeat the stroke on the other breast.

3 Gently squeeze a little skin at each side of your partner's nipple, and then very lightly slide outward toward the sides of her breast as though your fingers were moving along the spokes of a wheel to its rim. Repeat this stroke on all of the "spokes" of each nipple.

4 Squeeze your partner's nipple gently between a well-oiled forefinger and thumb, sliding them up and off it. For extra effect, you can use both hands alternately so that the action, and the sensations, are made continuous. Repeat on your partner's other nipple.

CUPPING THE BREASTS

When cupping the breasts, it is important to remember that they are glands, not muscles, and should not have heavy pressure applied to them.

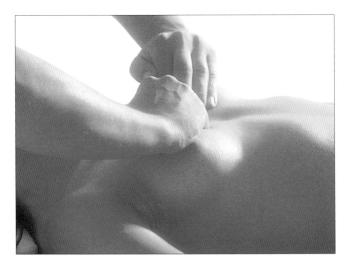

1 Starting at the breastbone and using the fingertips of both hands, make tiny circles over the whole of the upper chest, except the breasts.

2 Now cup your hands lightly under the breasts and gently sweep your palms and fingertips around them a few times.

3 Finally, increase your partner's level of excitement by gently brushing the ends of her nipples with your fingertips.

MASSAGING THE BELLY

THIS FORM OF MASSAGE can aid digestive processes and is very comforting. If your partner is one of those people whose belly is very ticklish, try making the moves slowly and firmly. Don't take your partner by surprise.

FINESSE IS THE KEY

Using the fingers of one hand, massage the belly with small circles. Work in a clockwise direction (the direction in which the colon runs), and then use your palm to massage in a large circle around the outer rim of the belly.

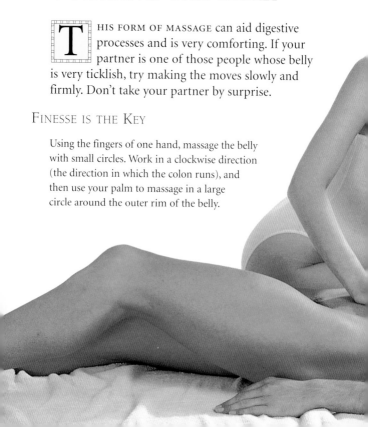

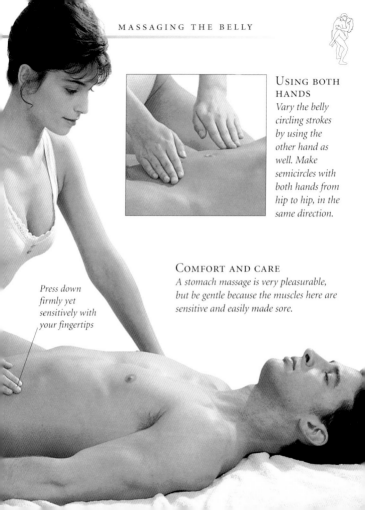

USING BOTH HANDS

Vary the belly circling strokes by using the other hand as well. Make semicircles with both hands from hip to hip, in the same direction.

COMFORT AND CARE

A stomach massage is very pleasurable, but be gentle because the muscles here are sensitive and easily made sore.

Press down firmly yet sensitively with your fingertips

KNEADING

This technique should be performed on the front of the body using both hands and focusing on the fleshy areas around the waist and the hips.

Use both hands simultaneously or alternately, and once you've covered all the suitably fleshy areas, vary the sensation by making circling motions with the tips of all the fingers. Don't knead bony areas where the skin is tight over the flesh – it can be painful.

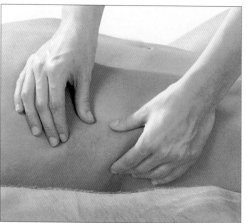

CONTINUITY
Work your thumbs and fingers in close conjunction over your partner's body to provide a complete, rolling set of varying sensations.

HAND TWISTING

Continue clockwise circles with one hand, only this time twist the hand itself for part of its run so that you are then massaging with the back of the hand.

Bend your fingers and the back of your hand over and around your partner's torso, being careful not to press too hard but varying the sensations as much as possible. If you have long nails, be careful not to scratch your partner.

KNUCKLE PRESSURE
Use your knuckles to vary the pressure and the whole feel of the massage as you work the back of your hand over your partner's torso.

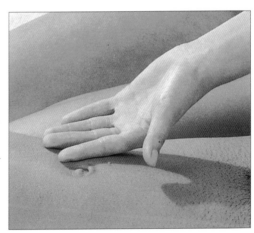

THE ABDOMINAL SLIDE

This is a wonderfully soothing stroke, but it's invigorating and energizing at the same time. Before you start, straddle your partner's thighs, positioning your weight so that he is entirely comfortable before the massage commences.

Slide your hands gently but firmly up your partner's abdomen from groin to ribs. Place both palms on his lower abdomen, with your fingers pointing toward your partner's head. Then push your hands (do not lean on them because your weight would be too much for your partner to take) slowly up the abdomen until your fingertips meet the ribcage, then bring your hand down around the side of the body, back toward you. Repeat as desired.

COMFORT FIRST
Ensure that your partner is comfortable and happy with the positioning of your body weight before you begin the massage.

Press firmly with your fingertips before beginning the slide up your partner's torso

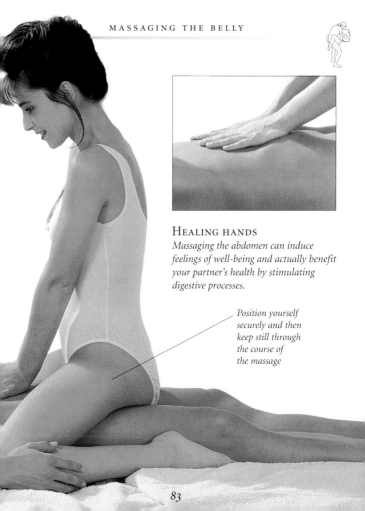

HEALING HANDS

Massaging the abdomen can induce feelings of well-being and actually benefit your partner's health by stimulating digestive processes.

Position yourself securely and then keep still through the course of the massage

THE ABDOMINAL TWIST

To vary the abdominal slide technique (*see page 82*), position your hands so that the heels of your palms face outward and the fingertips meet at your partner's middle. Gently sweep your hands apart below the ribcage so that your fingertips trace the bottom ribs.

- As with all other techniques, remove any rings before starting.
- Make sure your nails do not rake your partner's ribcage.
- Maintain a firm but sensitive pressure on your partner's abdomen throughout the massage.

FIND THE RIGHT TOUCH

It is very important that any tensions are properly eradicated through massage as they can inhibit the flow of sexual and vital energy that you must release to enjoy satisfying lovemaking.

- *The lighter you are able to make your touch, the more you will relax the emotional and physical tensions within your partner.*

- *Feel free to repeat strokes that your partner particularly enjoys. Use more surface strokes than deep layer ones, as these generate higher energy levels.*

CONSTANT TOUCH

An important rule of massage is that when you are giving someone full-body strokes, you should always try to have at least one hand in contact with your partner's skin. It is vital to maintain consistent contact between your hands and your partner's body, in order to generate the energy necessary to make the massage successful and fulfilling for the recipient.

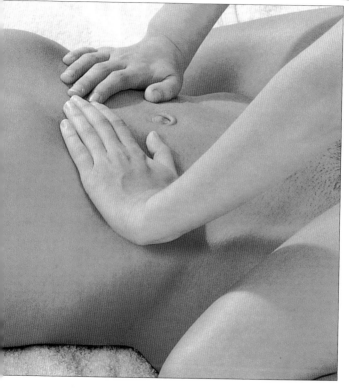

LEG MASSAGE

C OMPLETING A TASK is as important as beginning it, and the manner in which you complete something often reflects on the kind of person you are. If you're an impatient character, you might skimp the ending to get the job over and done with quickly. However, if you're a thoughtful personality, you might make the ending as lingering and as tactile as you did the beginning, and this is the approach to adopt for the leg massage, the final stage of a full-body massage.

TAKE YOUR TIME
The legs are just as important as any other part of the body, so treat them with the same respect.

Gentle squeezing with your thighs will enhance the overall experience of the massage

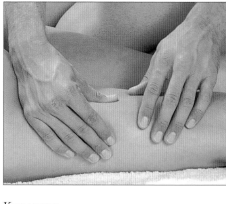

KNEADING

Using both hands, "knead" down the fleshy areas of the legs from the thighs down to the calves. Omit the backs of the knees.

Apply deep finger pressure by pushing down firmly with your fingertips

BODY CONTACT

W HEN YOU HAVE FINISHED massaging your
partner's back, head and shoulders, front, and
legs, it is time to move the whole experience on
from relaxation to arousal.

BODY CARESS

Lean forward onto your partner and sensuously slide your
body from side to side against his. Rub your chest against
his back and press your genitals against his buttocks.

FACE-TO-FACE
Full face-to-face body contact offers extra dimensions. The genitals are pressed together, and eye-to-eye contact enhances the experience.

Press your breasts against his back

Brush your hair against his body

GETTING CLOSER
The all-over sensation of a full body press induces powerful feelings of togetherness.

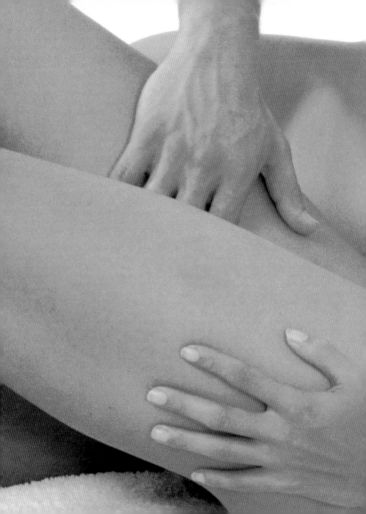

INTIMATE
TOUCH

No sensual massage would be complete without
proper attention being paid to the most
erogenous areas of the body and, in particular,
the genitals. They need preparing for
lovemaking as much as any other part of the
body, and the whole process of sexual energy
exchange will be more complete if you
embark on a long, lingering program of
intimate touch before making love.

EROTIC TOUCH
Women can enjoy high levels of arousal and achieve orgasm through erotic touch.

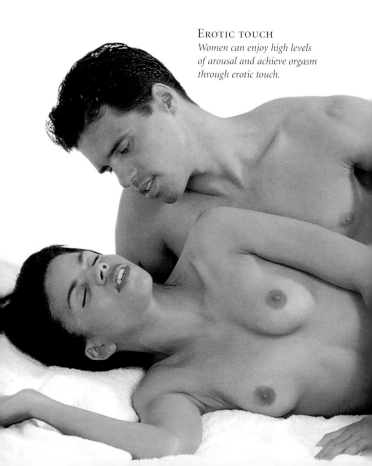

WHAT IS EROTICISM?

EROTIC TOUCH IS WHEN he strokes her forefinger, shooting molten desire through every pore. Erotic touch is when she casually grazes her lips across his until fire consumes his limbs. Eroticism always takes you by surprise. Eroticism is the sum of sweet talk and seduction, the quivering culmination of tease and tantalization. Eroticism is thought, innuendo, and finding out that your neurons are plugged directly into your lover's fingertips.

FOR HER PLEASURE

THIS MASSAGE, AND THE FOLLOWING ONE for men (*see page 96*), is based on techniques taught by Ray Stubbs, and also by graduates of the Institute for the Advanced Study of Human Sexuality in San Francisco. It is interesting to note that, while all of the strokes for men came with a title, none of the strokes for women had names, so I have christened them!

ASK HER
When you are masturbating your partner, ask her which touches she prefers.

Stroke the insides of her thighs first

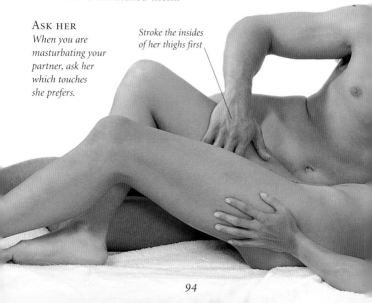

94

WIBBLING

Start with one of the outer labia. Using both your hands at the same time, gently pull on it, then let go, just as you might do if this were your bottom lip.

CLITORAL MANEUVERS

Extremely delicately, with an almost featherlight touch and using plenty of lubrication, run your finger first around the head and then up and down the shaft of her clitoris.

FOR HIS PLEASURE

WHEN MASSAGING your man's genitals, remember that you are not trying to bring him to orgasm. If it happens, it's a bonus for him, but if not, it really doesn't matter, because you will still have given him wonderful sensations. These are two of the more basic strokes I was originally taught, but there is nothing to stop you from inventing a few of your own, with a little practice and imagination.

THE LEMON SQUEEZER
Steady the penis by grasping it around the middle with one hand. Then rub the cupped palm of your other hand around the head of the penis, as if you were juicing a lemon.

HAND OVER HAND
Slide your cupped hand up over the head of the penis and down the shaft. Before it gets to the base, bring the other hand up to the head once more to repeat the stroke.

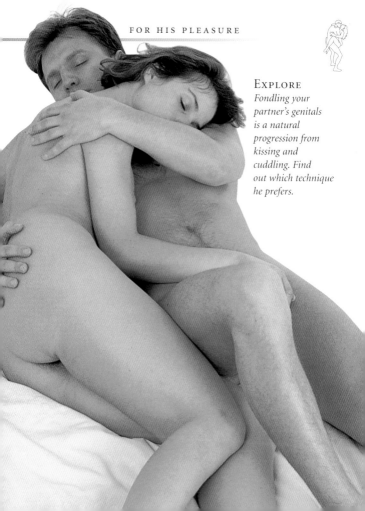

EXPLORE

*Fondling your
partner's genitals
is a natural
progression from
kissing and
cuddling. Find
out which technique
he prefers.*

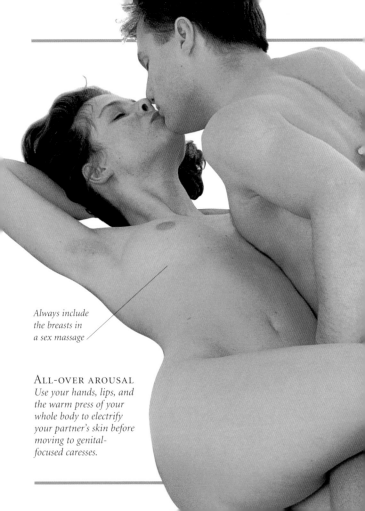

*Always include
the breasts in
a sex massage*

ALL-OVER AROUSAL
*Use your hands, lips, and
the warm press of your
whole body to electrify
your partner's skin before
moving to genital-
focused caresses.*

SEX MASSAGE

ONE OF THE TENETS OF A GOOD MASSAGE is that the masseur or masseuse should be completely trustworthy – that is, you could trust him or her to refrain from becoming sexual. (Sensual is not sexual.) But when you massage with a lover, the rules change. Sexual massage then has the opportunity of becoming an art form, as it is in the "Three-Handed Massage" techniques shown in this section. Naturally stimulating each other's genitals plays a large part in sexual massage, but it's vital to remember that this only works well if you have paid attention to the whole body first.

THE ULTIMATE TOUCH

Use an intimate massage as a sensational finale to the all-over attention you have paid previously. It is a highly arousing form of foreplay, and you will enjoy giving it almost as much as your partner will enjoy receiving it.

THREE-HANDED MASSAGE FOR HIM

American master of massage Ray Stubbs was the man responsible for sensitively developing the "Three–Handed Massage." His concept was to combine the relaxed sensuality of massage with the gentle touch of intercourse. The ancient Chinese believed that the penis and vagina contain certain meridian (energy) points. Ray used this idea to bring to life internal aspects of body electricity.

Take turns with this next exercise. The person massaged does not try to reciprocate simultaneously because their efforts will detract from the inner calm they might otherwise achieve.

SENSUAL SLIDING
Slide your well-oiled lower body all over your partner's buttocks and thighs before entering her.

SETTING UP THE MASSAGE

1 Give your partner 15 minutes or so of manual body massage, using the techniques shown earlier, before touching the genitals. Don't hurry. Take the strokes slowly and don't aim at orgasm – for either of you. After this manual massage, move onto step 2.

2 Give your lover a back massage and bring your legs across her thighs so that you are sitting on her. In order to have exceptionally smooth and slippery mobility, lavishly oil your own abdomen, genitals, and thighs.

3 Without interrupting your sensual massage of her body, let your well-oiled lower half glide backward and forward over her thighs and buttocks so that your genitals are in contact with her skin and, in effect, are also massaging her.

4 As you continue, let your penis find its slippery way between her slightly parted legs and make its own contact with her vagina. Allow yourself to penetrate her exceptionally slowly – and let your hands massage at the same time so that all the movements blend.

Three-Handed Massage for Her

The Three-Handed Massage works just as well the other way
around, too – that is, with the woman conducting the exercise.
The wonderful thing about this technique is that it can yield
as much pleasure for the giver as it does for the receiver.

How She Can Pleasure Him

1 Sit astride your partner with your thighs across his abdomen.
Begin by massaging his upper body, and then lean back to
massage as much of his thighs as you can reach. After doing this
for 15 minutes, lean over him and provocatively draw your
breasts over his chest, moving them up and down and from
side to side. The more oil you use, the more memorable the
breast-to-breast movement will be.

Complete pleasure
*Three-Handed Massage enables
you to give your partner a full
range of wonderful sensations.*

2 The next move is to slide your pelvis
slowly and gently across his penis.
Show your love by kissing and nuzzling
him as you do this. Once his penis stirs and
commences to grow, very, very slowly slide
yourself so that you can let your vagina
gradually slip against his penis until you have
genital contact without penetration. Gently rub
against his penis while continuing to massage with
your hands in a flowing and sensuous movement.
The secret of these special massages is to slow
everything down one hundred–fold.

Move your hands slowly and
provocatively over his body

SELF-TOUCH

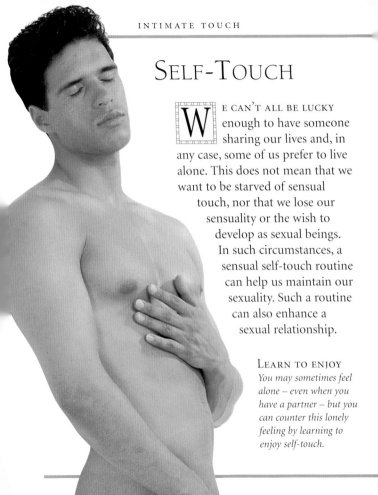

WE CAN'T ALL BE LUCKY enough to have someone sharing our lives and, in any case, some of us prefer to live alone. This does not mean that we want to be starved of sensual touch, nor that we lose our sensuality or the wish to develop as sexual beings. In such circumstances, a sensual self-touch routine can help us maintain our sexuality. Such a routine can also enhance a sexual relationship.

LEARN TO ENJOY
You may sometimes feel alone – even when you have a partner – but you can counter this lonely feeling by learning to enjoy self-touch.

SO MUCH TO FEEL

*Do not make the mistake
of thinking that self-touch
is all about masturbation:
there are so many different
techniques and areas
of your body you can
enjoy. Never feel guilty
about your preferred
kind of touch: self-
fulfillment is your goal.*

LOVING YOUR BODY

*To enjoy self-touch to the
full, it is essential to be
positive about your body.*

SELF-TOUCH FOR WOMEN

THIS EROTIC SELF-TOUCH ROUTINE is a particularly enjoyable way of exploring your own body and getting to know and appreciate it. By giving yourself such intimate and powerful sensations, you will be discovering your own preferences and dislikes when it comes to sensual touch.

ARMS

Pour a little oil into the palms of your hands and coat your forearms with it. Work it well into the skin, using powerful strokes, then stroke your forearms gently and lovingly with your fingers. Now repeat the exercise on your upper arms.

Try out different kinds of strokes until you find the ones you like best

SELF-APPRECIATION
No matter how you touch yourself, enjoy your body and treat it with respect.

FONDLING YOUR BREASTS
Experiment with a range of different strokes and caresses as you feel your breasts. Amazing sensations can be enjoyed.

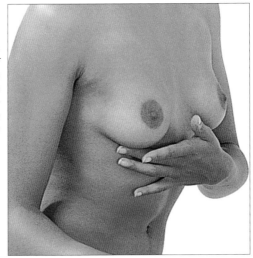

BREASTS

With warm, well-oiled hands, fondle and caress your breasts and move them in circles, paying attention to the bottoms and sides as well as to the tops and fronts. Then gently knead and squeeze them, first one at a time and then both together. Note which kind of touch feels best.

BELOW THE WAIST

Do not confine your self-touch to your breasts. You can awaken a range of wonderful sensations by experimenting with touch on different parts of your body, particularly below your waist.

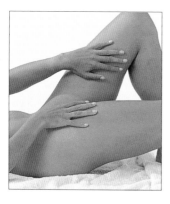

INSIDES OF THIGHS
After massaging your buttocks, roll over onto your back and, without touching your genitals, stroke and fondle the insides of your thighs. Vary the pressure and speed of the strokes as you run your hands up and down.

OUTSIDES OF THIGHS
Slowly roll over onto one side and make yourself comfortable. Massage the outside of your uppermost thigh from your buttock down to your knee. Then roll onto your other side and repeat on the other thigh.

BUTTOCKS

*While lying on your front or side, stroke your buttocks
with your fingertips and the palms of your hands, using
large, circular, swirling movements.*

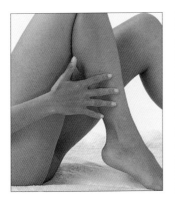

CALVES

*Lie on your back and run your
hands up the backs and sides of
your calves, squeezing gently with
your fingers and thumbs. Work
repeatedly from the ankle up to
the knee and back again.*

GENITALS

*Finally, close your eyes and begin to
lovingly caress and fondle your
genitals. Slowly explore them with
your fingers, starting with the labia
and vagina and then moving on to
stimulate your clitoris.*

SELF-TOUCH FOR MEN

FOR THIS ROUTINE, arrange to have at least an hour of uninterrupted privacy. Begin by giving yourself a warm bath or shower; a bath is preferable, since it is more relaxing. Then move to a warm room, take the telephone off the hook, and lock the door.

THE HANDS AND ARMS

Begin by massaging a little warmed oil from one hand to the other. Next, massage the back of each hand, then move on to your arms. Use powerful strokes up and down each arm, then squeeze the arm by the wrist and push your hand up to the elbow. Follow these firm strokes with more gentle touching.

Finish by touching and stroking yourself lovingly

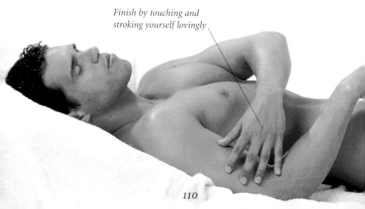

THE CHEST AND NIPPLES

Apply the massage oil with both hands and move them in circles all over your chest except on the nipples, covering a small area at a time. Then apply a little fresh oil to each of your nipples, and gently stroke, squeeze, and fondle them to find out what it feels like. The nipples are a very sensitive part of the body and you might find touching them highly erotic.

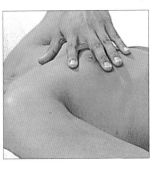

CHANGING STROKES
Grade the strokes and circles you make on your chest, treating your nipples more sensitively.

RELAX AND ENJOY
The more you can relax and clear your mind, the more you will be able to concentrate on and enjoy the feel of your self-touch.

BELOW THE WAIST

Intimate self-touch works on all parts of the body, not just the torso. There are areas below the waist that will respond to sensitive touch and provide a range of wonderful feelings.

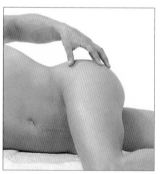

THE ABDOMEN
Oil your hands and move them firmly in short, circular strokes over your abdomen, repeatedly working down from your waist to your groin and back. Use a combination of firm and light strokes.

THE THIGHS
Stroke repeatedly up your thighs from your knees to your genitals, covering both the outsides and the insides of your legs with firm motions. Do not be tempted to touch your genitals at this stage.

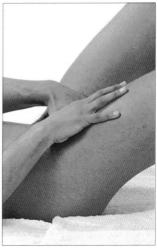

THE LOWER LEG

Stroke each leg in turn, working repeatedly from the ankle up to the knee and back again, being careful not to jab the sensitive back of the knee. You may find that your anklebone is a surprisingly erotic area.

THE PENIS

Close your eyes and begin to lightly stroke your penis, but not as you would during masturbation. Take your time as you experiment, noting the texture of your penis and how it feels to your hand.

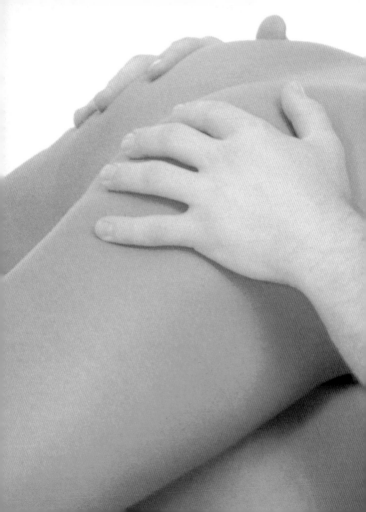

PROLONGING THE PLEASURE

Take time over your lovemaking – learn to
prolong the experience and enjoy it to the full.
The Taoist and Tantric masters of ancient China
and India believed that our bodies are steeped in
a rich and infinite source of energy that finds its
greatest expression in prolonged lovemaking.
They taught that the release of sexual energy
should be a gradual process, leading to sexual
satisfaction and complete self-fulfillment.

AN ECSTATIC UNION

To ACHIEVE TRUE SEXUAL ECSTASY, you have to be completely at one with your partner. Spend time exploring and enjoying each other; revel in your nakedness; kiss, touch, and caress the whole of your partner's body; feel the electrifying energy that engulfs your bodies. Building this powerful union of bodies and minds before you begin full intercourse, will bring you to extremes of intimacy and pleasure.

PREPARING FOR LOVE

There are several ways to lead into and prolong the pleasure of lovemaking. This chapter explores the simple pleasures of kissing and foreplay, and reveals some of the ancient Eastern sexual secrets that will enable you and your lover to build your energy levels to a peak, and enjoy heightened sexual pleasure.

TUNING INTO YOUR PARTNER

This ancient Chinese visualization technique helps lovers unite sexual energy.

1 Picture your lover's naked body. Imagine tiny tongues of flame erupting from every pore. The skin is bathed in a hovering haze of fire that soon becomes transparent, like a summer haze.

2 Place your hand above your lover's skin. The tiny, invisible flames are sucked into your hands, they flicker up your arms and out along your shoulders. Soon your entire skin is burning invisibly, as is your lover's – you are linked by a picture of a consuming, yet heatless fire.

BECOMING ONE
By taking the time to tune into each other, you and your partner will enjoy a truly intimate and special lovemaking experience.

KISSING

A KISS CAN BE many different things – a greeting, an expression of love, or an essential part of foreplay and lovemaking in general. Since the lips and tongue are among the most sensitive parts of the body, gentle, tender kissing and deep kissing alike can be as erotic as sex itself. Never underestimate the power and importance of the kiss in your lovemaking.

KISS WITH CONFIDENCE
Skillful kissing will enhance your own emotional state and build your partner's confidence and excitement levels, too.

INTIMACY
Kissing at the height of lovemaking is intimate and moving. It is as private and special as any other aspect of sex.

SENSUAL FOREPLAY

T O AWAKEN SEXUAL DESIRE GRADUALLY it's essential that you don't rush into intercourse. Sensual foreplay techniques – from tantalizing touch to soft kisses and caresses – will start to arouse your partner gently. Use your hands, lips, and tongue to explore and enjoy every inch of your lover's body and discover the most erogenous zones.

Slowly work down your lover's body with kisses and caresses

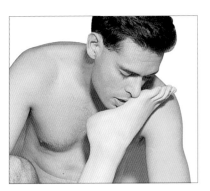

TAKE YOUR TIME

Arouse your lover by exploring every inch of her body, and discover the touches, kisses, and caresses that give the most pleasure.

TANTALIZING TOUCH

Once you begin to stimulate the area around the genitals, you will rapidly arouse your partner's sexual desire.

THE SETS OF NINE

FOOT REFLEXOLOGISTS BELIEVE that by applying stimulation to nerve endings in the foot, they can energize related organs. There are similar nerve endings – or reflexology zones – in the penis and vagina. The "Sets of Nine" (*see page 125*) is a Taoist exercise designed to massage these genital reflexology zones evenly and thus benefit the rest of the body.

The body parts affected – the "Seven Glands" – are the pineal, the pituitary, the thyroid, the thymus, the pancreas, the adrenal glands, and the sexual glands (prostate and testes in the man and ovaries in the female).

Only squeeze gently, or he may ejaculate before completing the Sets of Nine

INTERNAL MASSAGE

The folds of the vaginal canal and the uneven shape of the penis make it difficult to evenly massage the penis or vagina during regular intercourse. The Sets of Nine exercise – one complete Set of Nine being a total of 90 strokes – aims to put this right.

Serious students should aim at more than one set, although it can take a lot of practice to master the technique without ejaculating.

"INJACULATION"

The Taoist technique of "injaculation" using the Jen-Mo point (*see page 137*) can be used in conjunction with the Sets of Nine, both for its beneficial effect on the man's health and for its usefulness in helping him to prolong intercourse.

— By taking your weight on your arms, you can control thrusting more effectively

INTERNAL MASSAGE
The Sets of Nine are believed by some to give energy through internal massage to the vagina and penis.

CARRYING OUT THE SETS OF NINE

It's important to understand that this is not intercourse for pleasure alone. The activity may feel arousing, but the principle here is that you are taking a preventative health measure with the result that the "Seven Glands" are energized (*see previous page*).

Perhaps the most important preliminary for a long lovemaking session is that you should feel comfortable while doing it. To this end, decide on the most easeful place and ensure there will be no interruptions. Take the phone off the hook, lock the door, and ensure that anything you may need is within reach.

FOCUS ON YOUR GOAL
You should enjoy performing the Sets of Nine, but remember, they are designed primarily to benefit your health.

THE SETS OF NINE

The key action in this activity is thrusting and this is
thrusting done with a great deal of bodily control.
The Sets of Nine are therefore best carried out from a
man-on-top position. The following 90 deep and shallow
strokes need to be done in order:

1 *He thrusts only the penis
head into the vagina before
withdrawing. He does this
shallow stroke nine times, and
then he thrusts the entire penis
into the vagina once.*

2 *He follows this up with eight of
the shallow strokes (penetrating
with the penis head only) and
two deep strokes (penetrating
with the entire penis).*

3 *Next, he makes seven shallow
strokes and three deep ones.*

4 *Six shallow strokes followed by
four deep ones.*

5 *Five shallow strokes and five
deep ones.*

6 *Four shallow strokes and six
deep ones.*

7 *Three shallow strokes and
seven deep ones.*

8 *Two shallow strokes and eight
deep ones.*

9 *Finally, he makes one shallow
stroke followed by nine deep ones.*

*A word of advice: if you want to carry out further sets, check
with your partner first that she really wants this. Thrusting for
the sake of thrusting may have an important purpose, but you
can also have too much of a good thing.
Use your common sense!*

DEER EXERCISE FOR HER

ANCIENT CHINESE PHILOSOPHERS perceived that the deer, noted for its strong reproductive activities, exercised its anus when it wiggled its tail. They developed a "tail-wiggling" concept, to increase sexual arousal in men and women, and called it the Deer Exercise. Women can also adapt this technique by exercising their pelvic floor muscles, which in turn evokes erotic feelings.

GETTING PREPARED

To prepare for the Deer Exercise, sit cross-legged on the bed, get as comfortable as possible, and focus your mind. Make sure that your hands are well warmed.

PERFECT SELF-TOUCH

Self-touch should be enjoyed as completely and in as guilt-free a manner as possible. When it is done confidently, with total relaxation in mind, it can yield pleasures as great as those that can be enjoyed in lovemaking with another person.

BREAST MASSAGE

Begin your sexual arousal with slow, sensual breast massage. Stroke your breasts slowly with circular movements. The movement is counterclockwise on the right breast, clockwise on the left. Massage your breasts this way at least 36 times and at most 360 in the morning and again in the evening.

Run your fingers smoothly under the curve of your breasts

CONCENTRATE ON THE FEELING

As you stroke and massage your breasts, feel their contours and focus hard on their texture and mass.

VAGINAL PRESSURE

Sit cross-legged with the heel of one foot pressed up against your vaginal entrance. If this is difficult, place a small ball between your foot and vagina. The pressure from heel or ball stimulates sexual feelings and releases sexual energy.

HUMAN DEER

We may not have tails to wiggle, but stimulating the muscles in the anal and vaginal areas has the same effect.

Press your heel against your vaginal opening

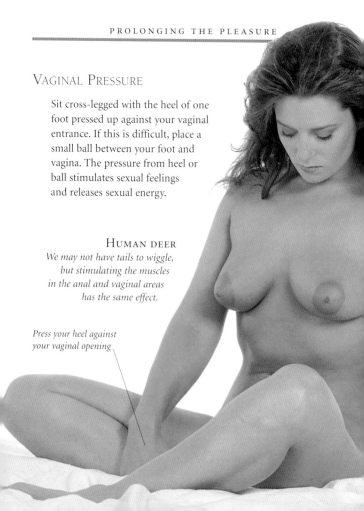

ALL-OVER PLEASURE
As you contract your vagina and anus, you should experience a deep and satisfying feeling traveling up through your spine, right to your ears.

DRAWING UP ENERGY

Massage each breast in turn with one hand, using the other hand to press your vaginal opening. Contract the muscles in your vagina and anus as if you were trying to control your flow of urine, then focus hard on contracting the anus further. Hold, then relax, and repeat 20 times. To check that you are doing it properly, insert a finger into the vagina to see if you can grip it, or at least tighten on it.

DEER EXERCISE FOR HIM

THE DEER EXERCISE works just as effectively for men as it does for women, and – at least according to the Taoists – offers the added bonus of increasing the production of semen. Whether this is the case or not, the exercise is always soothing and relaxing.

FACILITATING SEMEN PRODUCTION

Sitting cross-legged, cup your testicles gently in one hand and place the flat of the other hand on your abdomen, just below the navel. Using a circular motion, massage the left side of your abdomen 81 times, and then repeat on the right side. The pressure exerted on both your testicles and your abdomen should not be too great. Make sure you are comfortable with both the handling and the massaging.

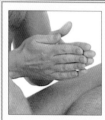

WARM HANDS
The Deer Exercise involves self-massage so, before you begin, it's a good idea to make sure that your hands are warm, either by rubbing them vigorously together or by washing them in hot water.

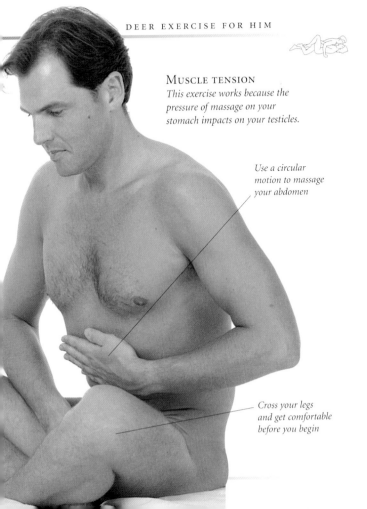

MUSCLE TENSION

This exercise works because the pressure of massage on your stomach impacts on your testicles.

Use a circular motion to massage your abdomen

Cross your legs and get comfortable before you begin

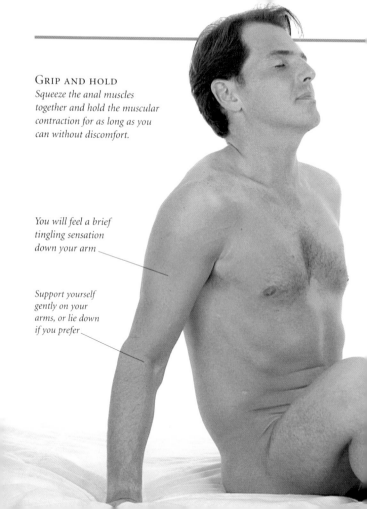

GRIP AND HOLD
Squeeze the anal muscles together and hold the muscular contraction for as long as you can without discomfort.

You will feel a brief tingling sensation down your arm

Support yourself gently on your arms, or lie down if you prefer

PROSTATE MASSAGE

This simple and discreet technique exercises the anal muscles which in turn massage the prostate gland.

Squeeze the anal muscles together and hold as tightly as you comfortably can. Relax for a minute, then repeat. Do this as many times as you can without discomfort. You can do this anywhere, be it in the privacy of the bath or walking in the country. Taoist teachers say that anal contractions, which stimulate the prostate gland, produce enhanced hormonal secretion and a natural high.

SIT OR STAND?
You can benefit your prostate gland with regular anal contraction in any position and at any time.

TAOIST TEACHINGS
The Taoist thinkers of ancient China were interested in the spiritual and metaphysical aspects of sexual congress, much like the Tantric theorists of India. Tao teachings also embraced the medical benefits of sexual exercise.

NINE LEVELS OF ORGASM

WE IGNORANT WESTERNERS have little understanding of the quality of a woman's orgasm. Even though clinical observation shows that women experience climaxes consisting of many differing lengths and strengths, in a variety of body sites, somehow this has taken its time to filter through to the ordinary man and woman in bed.

OPENING UP

Ancient Tao sexology describes a woman's orgasms as a series of upwardly rising steps followed by one declining step. These steps actually flow together, each step overlapping and building on the previous one.

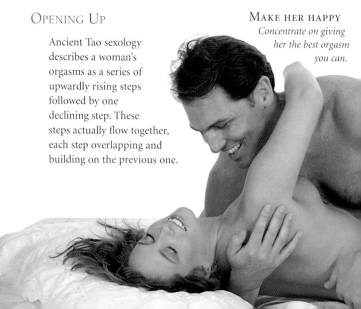

MAKE HER HAPPY
Concentrate on giving her the best orgasm you can.

THE NINE LEVELS

Each level of orgasm energizes certain parts of the body and evokes certain observable and predictable responses in the woman.

◆ *Level One (lungs): the woman sighs, breathes deeply, and salivates.*

◆ *Level Two (heart): while kissing the man, she extends her tongue out to him.*

◆ *Level Three (spleen, pancreas, stomach): as her muscles become activated, she grasps him tightly.*

◆ *Level Four (kidneys and bladder): she experiences a series of vaginal spasms at this time and secretions begin to flow.*

◆ *Level Five (bone): her joints loosen and she bites her partner.*

◆ *Level Six (liver and nerves): she undulates like a snake, trying to wrap her arms and legs around him.*

◆ *Level Seven (blood): her blood is "boiling" and she is frantically trying to touch her man everywhere.*

◆ *Level Eight (muscles): her muscles completely relax. She bites even more and grabs frantically at his nipples.*

◆ *Level Nine (entire body): she collapses in a "little death," surrendering to her partner.*

EXPERIENCING NEW LEVELS OF PLEASURE

Most Western women will have experienced the first four levels, but to reach the heights of the remaining five, the man must continue to stimulate his partner when she has reached orgasm: he should not stop.

MAKING LOVE LAST LONGER

THE TAOIST BELIEF is that prolonged intercourse is desirable because it ensures that the sexual batteries are recharged. But sometimes the sheer excitement of all that wonderful feeling coursing through the body, as every inch of you touches and rubs against every inch of your partner, proves too much. Regardless of your desires or of your "higher" feelings, a sensational sex session comes to an end for perfectly delightful reasons. This is why the Taoists invented the Jen-Mo exercise – a method by which the man delays his orgasm by "injaculating" his semen.

CONTINUING BLISS

The Jen-Mo technique enables you to make the heights of lovemaking last as long as possible.

THE JEN-MO POINT TECHNIQUE

The Jen-Mo point technique involves putting pressure on a sensitive spot located between the anus and the scrotum at the very moment orgasm approaches.

Pressing the Jen-Mo point is easy. Simply reach out behind you at the appropriate moment, and press so that the seminal fluid is not allowed to travel through the urethra. You may like to practice this in private first. The pressure should be neither too firm nor too soft. If you apply the pressure too close to the anus, the move won't work. If you press too close to the scrotum, the semen will go into the bladder rather than the bloodstream and make your urine cloudy when you urinate.

DON'T HOLD ON TOO LONG

Despite the ancient belief that the expulsion of bodily fluids results in a loss of energy, I happen to believe that constantly building up sexual tension and then giving it nowhere to go is bad for you. In my view, sexual tension amounts to bodily energy, and energy needs a point of dispersal. So never go on for too long, and do allow yourself to climax in the end. Apart from preventing your own complete satisfaction, choosing not to ejaculate could offend your partner, who might view it as an act of withholding. Creating relationship problems is not part of sexual enjoyment.

HELP FROM YOUR PARTNER

By using the squeeze technique (see opposite), your partner can help to delay your orgasm and prolong the pleasure for both of you.

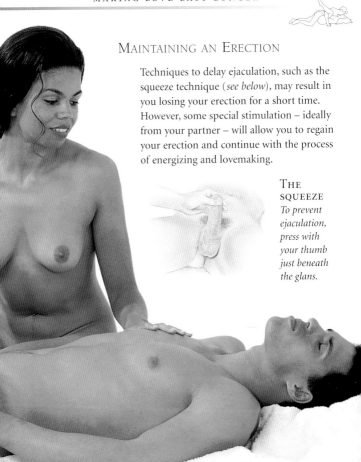

MAINTAINING AN ERECTION

Techniques to delay ejaculation, such as the squeeze technique (*see below*), may result in you losing your erection for a short time. However, some special stimulation – ideally from your partner – will allow you to regain your erection and continue with the process of energizing and lovemaking.

THE SQUEEZE

To prevent ejaculation, press with your thumb just beneath the glans.

ENERGY FOR A DAY

WE ARE POOR AT TAKING TIME OFF to nourish our bodies. And yet, all of us have a need to do this regularly. The following is a touch program for one day only which, when practiced once a week or so, will rejuvenate you and give you greater peace of mind.

WAKING UP

Take your time over waking. Snuggle, spoons-fashion, for at least 15 minutes. Revel in the sense and smell of each other. If you normally leap out of bed first thing and throw back the drapes, don't.

FIRST STAGE

After eating a light breakfast and visiting the bathroom, sit opposite each other, close together. Lightly stroke each other, with a circling action. Avoid the breasts and genitals and spend at least 15 minutes on caressing. Take a brief break, then repeat for another 15 minutes. After completing this first stage, lie quietly together in the spoons position, enjoying each other's closeness. Listen for each other's heartbeat.

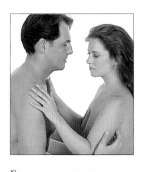

FEEL THE CLOSENESS
Don't just sit close together – get close together – by concentrating your minds and enjoying each other's presence.

Snuggle close together in the spoons position

LIE QUIETLY
Give yourselves time to relax properly and give your bodies a break. Lie quietly together and savor the moment.

SECOND STAGE

Sit opposite each other again and stroke once
more, only this time include the breasts. Continue
to leave the genitals out. Then rest again.

SKILLFUL
HANDLING
*Vary the pace and
pressure of your
stroking to give your
partner a truly
memorable breast
massage.*

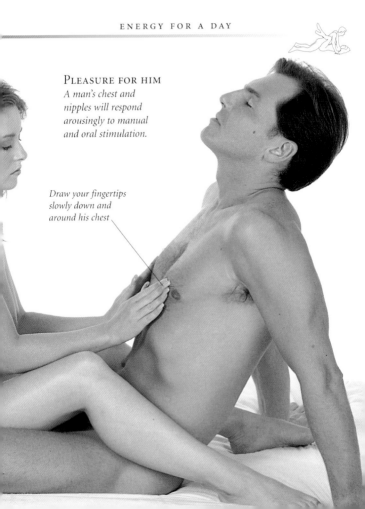

PLEASURE FOR HIM
A man's chest and nipples will respond arousingly to manual and oral stimulation.

Draw your fingertips slowly down and around his chest

RAISE THE STAKES

Bring the massage to its natural climax by moving your hands gently and tantalizingly to the genitals, using light, lingering strokes on and around them.

THIRD STAGE

Continue with the massage, but this time include the genitals, drawing the fingers around and underneath them, lightly but lingeringly. This is not meant to end in orgasm. Then rest again.

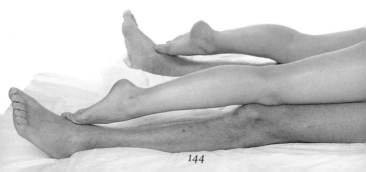

FINAL STAGE

Massage again, on this occasion spending at least an hour on genital stroking. Then take a five-minute break. Now lie motionless, with her on top and your penis in her vagina until your erection subsides. Then rest in the spoons position again.

Repeat the last stage, only, on this occasion, take it to its ultimate conclusion, reveling in the pleasures of mutual orgasm.

Done at a relaxed pace, the program can last the day. You may want to include a light lunch somewhere in the proceedings. And if you find part of the afternoon is free, go for a walk together. But stay apart from the rest of the world until the evening, relishing your closeness and the intimacy of what you have experienced.

Stroke and comfort your partner as you lie together

ULTIMATE TOGETHERNESS
There is nothing to compare with the complete feeling of intimacy that this program can engender.

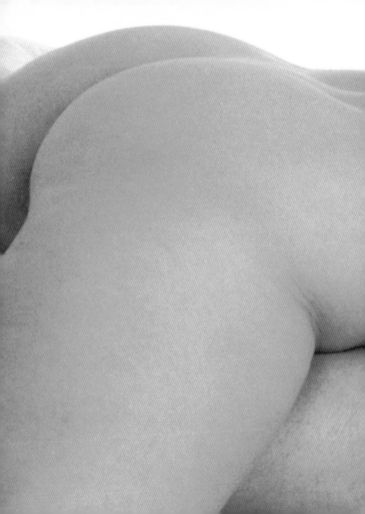

SEXUAL
POSITIONS

There are countless different sexual positions to
be enjoyed, and it is good to experiment and find
the ones that suit you and your partner best.
Great sexual positions have always been
celebrated – from the classic Indian erotic work
Kama Sutra to the Arabic *Perfumed Garden*, every
conceivable variation of human sexual congress
has been recorded. The pages that follow describe
some of the very best positions of all.

MAKING LOVE

THERE ARE LOVEMAKING POSITIONS which generate so much skin electricity that you end up giving off great clouds of energy in the form of heat. Some of the most exhilarating lovemaking sessions are those where fiery body meets fiery body, transforming lovers into incandescent meteors, crashing toward the shock of cosmic explosion.

CHOOSE WISELY

Of course, in order to reach these heights, you need to be fit. Energy conservation is the opposite of energy generation, and older people, or less-fit lovers, must make energy conservation a priority. Accordingly, this section describes methods that generate maximum energy as well as love positions that conserve energy.

Use your leg to pull your partner toward you

ENJOY YOURSELVES

If you have by now experimented with massage and other foreplay techniques, you may choose to incorporate some of these activities in the sex position suggestions that appear on the following pages. But there are no rules to sex. It is always up to you, the individual, what you choose to do. Never feel constrained to act out something sexual because you think you "ought."

Your thrusting can bring ecstasy to your partner

Enjoy yourself, but consider your partner's needs

BE REALISTIC

Do what you can enjoy in comfort – don't try to be a sexual superhuman.

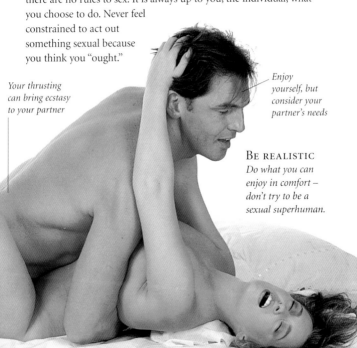

WOMAN ON TOP

SKIN UPON SKIN creates sensations of wallowing in sensuality; some of the very best lovemaking can be achieved when one's full body is pressed against the other. But as a lead-in to such all-immersion scenarios, here are some of the more athletic love positions in which she builds up body tension. Positions that are especially effective are those where tension is centered around the pelvis and gained through tantalizing each other in upright sex maneuvers.

BASIC POSITION
This straightforward woman-on-top position is great for deep thrusting and building tension.

THE HORSE OF HECTOR

In this woman-on-top position, her knees are placed each side of him. She sits up during penetration and then leans back, using his raised knees for support. This position is excellent for deep penetration.

Maximize contact by stroking and holding him

THE LYONS STAGECOACH

In this position, she sits on her partner's penis with her legs toward (or even over) his shoulders while leaning back on her hands.

LOVING CONTACT

Lying prone on top of him allows you to use your entire body to show him your love and affection.

PLEASURING YOUR PARTNER

Using your hands, lips, hair, and breasts can arouse an explosion of sensations in your man which will affect far more than his genital area. The beauty of woman-on-top positions is that they allow you to exert such positive control over your partner – a control that can give you an intense thrill while pleasuring him to the utmost.

Press your breasts against his chest

Tell your partner your sexual desires

TAKING THE LEAD

The rhythm of sexual intercourse gathers new shape when a woman takes over. Not only can you better ensure your own stimulation, but you can also allow lovemaking to take on new directions. One way in which you can tease your man is to promise intercourse, but then withhold it up until the very last moment, drawing away from him even as you allow the head of his penis to slip inside.

Where your own eroticism is concerned, the woman-on-top position allows your clitoris to get the attention it deserves through the subtle control of well-positioned thrusting.

BEING IN CONTROL

Enjoy the experience of gently dominating your partner, controlling the pace of proceedings, and introducing new variations as you ride him.

A dominant body position is powerful and arousing

Holding down his hands makes him feel submissive

UPRIGHT FROM BEHIND
In this version of the back-to-front, woman-on-top position, it is easy to reach down and fondle his testicles.

Stroke her clitoris as you thrust

RIDE A COCK HORSE
Sink down deep onto your partner's penis, melding your buttocks with his stomach. Lean back against him for support.

BACK TO FRONT

Woman-on-top positions afford wonderful
versatility for both partners – there
are so many variations. One highly
erotic and novel alternative is
the back-to-front variety,
which enables deep
penetration and easy
access to her clitoris.

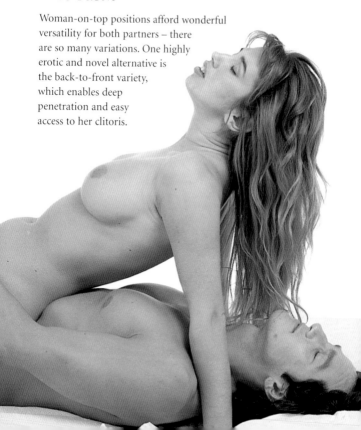

MAN ON TOP

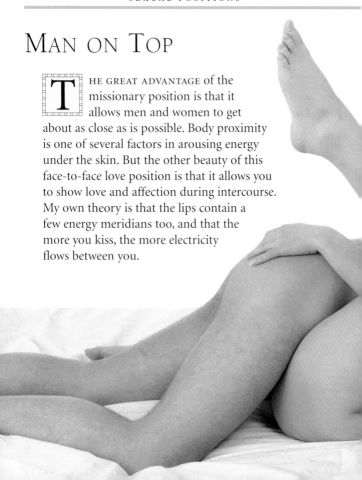

T HE GREAT ADVANTAGE of the missionary position is that it allows men and women to get about as close as is possible. Body proximity is one of several factors in arousing energy under the skin. But the other beauty of this face-to-face love position is that it allows you to show love and affection during intercourse. My own theory is that the lips contain a few energy meridians too, and that the more you kiss, the more electricity flows between you.

THE MISSIONARY

The missionary position is so-called because, allegedly, missionaries sent out to "civilize" the old imperial colonies thought it was the only respectable position for decent people and insisted that their converts use it.

TAKING THE STRAIN

In a face-to-face position such as the missionary, your full weight bears down on your partner. Make sure you reduce the pressure on her by holding yourself up as much as possible with your arms.

FUN TIME

Some of the most fun in lovemaking comes when you roll around like puppies, letting wild movements take you all over the bed.

VARIATIONS ON A THEME

One of the joys of the man-on-top positions is the number of variations it offers. Most of these involve the woman altering the position of her legs – for example, she might put them straight out in front of her so that her man is almost trapped between her legs, creating greater friction. But she may also wrap her legs around her lover's body, or draw her feet up toward her chest, enabling him to penetrate her deeply.

COMFORT COUNTS

*Deep thrusting will move
her around a lot, so try
these positions on soft,
comfortable surfaces and be
careful of carpet burn.*

GOING IN DEEP

*Whenever your legs –
either one or both – are
elevated toward your
shoulders, deep penetration
is guaranteed.*

*Support your
weight on
your arms*

TEASE AND TEMPT

As well as being affectionate, in a
face-to-face position, you can excite with
suggestive remarks and expressions.

*Thrust deeply against
her raised pelvis*

SHOWING AFFECTION

Perhaps the greatest advantage of face-to-face positions like this, whether man on top or woman on top, is that they allow you to be affectionate to each other. Eye-to-eye contact, kissing, nuzzling, and whispering sweet nothings are all so much easier face-to-face!

Pull him toward you as you raise your hips

CARESS WITH WORDS
Sweet, warm talk means so much to a partner at the height of lovemaking.

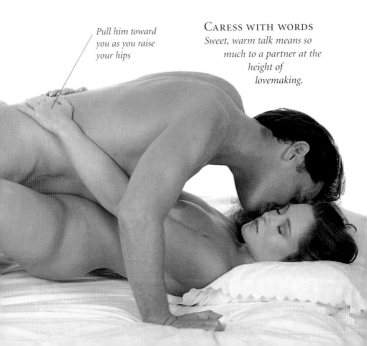

CARE AND CONSIDERATION
The woman is very vulnerable in this position. The man should be gentle and careful.

Push her legs back as far as they will go comfortably

DEEP PENETRATION

For a man-on-top position that enables really deep penetration, you should lie on your back and bring your knee right up toward your chin, so that when he enters you, your feet are at each side of his head. When you are using this position, which is advisable only if you are really supple and fit and not prone to back problems, he should be careful not to hurt you and a little cautious in his thrusting, because of the deep penetration possible. With care, deep thrusting can be intensely erotic and exciting.

BUILD ON THE EXPERIENCE

In this position you can increase your partner's pleasure by stroking and massaging the backs of her thighs, her vulva, and her clitoris, all of which are easily accessible when her legs are thrown back so far.

SIDE BY SIDE

SEXUAL INTERCOURSE EXPENDS ENERGY. A great deal of strength is used by the person on top. Couples can conserve energy by adopting a more restful approach. Lying side by side while lovemaking is normally energy-conserving and gentle. Try lying face-to-face, in the spoons position, or spread out in the scissors position. One of the other advantages of side-by-side lovemaking positions is that it is possible to use strong thigh friction to give both the penis and the vagina extra stimulation.

EASY DOES IT
*Side-by-side positions
are perfect for slow,
sensuous lovemaking.*

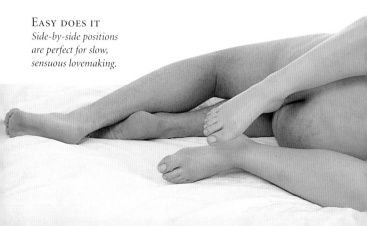

VARIETY IS FUN

As with the missionary, the side-by-side, face-to-face position has many possible variations. Here, she has one leg between his and one wrapped around his back. This enables the couple to vary the depth of penetration.

Lovingly caress your partner's back

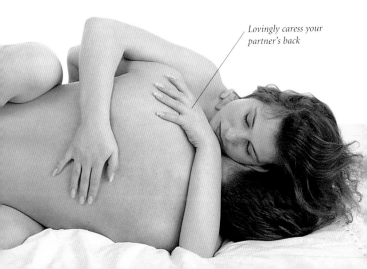

CHANGE THE PACE

It is easy for the man to control the depth, speed, and frequency of his thrusting in most side-by-side positions, because he is fully supported on one side.

Massage your partner's buttocks with your free hand as you move back and forth

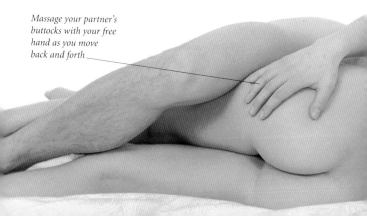

LOVING SIDE BY SIDE

Lovemaking side by side offers tremendous scope for variety. There is a sort of "weightlessness" to the positions, because you are never pinned beneath your partner when lying in this way. By repositioning your legs frequently, you can change the angle and depth of penetration at will, while enjoying the intimacy of full face-to-face contact.

SATISFACTION GUARANTEED
Lovemaking side by side is deeply intimate and fulfilling because it enables face-to-face proximity without the pressure of one body on top of another.

Lovingly caress the back of his neck

TENDER LOVING

Make the most of the closeness of side-by-side positions. Tell your partner how you feel, how much you care, and exactly what you are experiencing as you make love. Intimate interaction of this kind will join you emotionally and add powerfully to the eroticism of the experience.

KISSES AND CARESSES
The experience of side-by-side lovemaking can be richly enhanced by the many opportunities it offers for kissing and caressing.

Stroke and caress his arms for greater intimacy

Grip him tightly with your thighs for extra stimulation

TALK ABOUT IT

Take advantage of the intimacy of this position by telling each other what you are feeling as you make love.

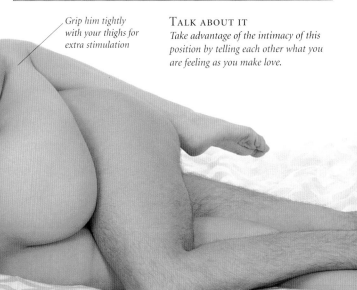

SITTING POSITIONS

ALTHOUGH SITTING POSITIONS do not provide the fastest means of achieving orgasm, like side-by-side positions they promote intimacy and closeness because of their symmetrical, face-to-face nature. Neither partner is required to take the dominant role, and there are plenty of variations on the theme to keep things fun and interesting.

LEANING APART
By leaning back and taking the weight on your hands, you can move more easily.

SITTING ASTRIDE

In this position, you can press the whole of your upper body against your partner.

SEATED POSITIONS

The delight of fooling
around erotically while
seated means that he
can increase sensation
for her by stroking
her genitals with his
fingertips, while
she encloses
his penis.

*Wrap your legs
seductively over his* ———

SEATED
SIDEWAYS-ON
*If she turns sideways,
he will find it easy
to stimulate her
genitals with
sensitive fingers.*

SEATED FACE-TO-FACE

If you are supple, you can make this highly erotic position part of a sequence: from sitting, you can move to a standing position, and then to a kneeling position. Finish in a man-on-top position.

SEATED FACING AWAY

The man can't move too much in this position except to reach up and caress his partner's breasts. The woman can take some of her weight and set the tempo by sitting forward and facing away from him.

REAR-ENTRY POSITIONS

VAGINAL PENETRATION FROM BEHIND can be in a standing, sitting, kneeling, or lying position, and it doesn't have to mean that the man is dominant. There are several positions in which the woman can take the lead and control the sexual tempo.

SUPPORTED "DOGGIE"
In this position, by opening your legs wide, you can present your upturned vagina invitingly.

Rest your weight on your arms, leaning on soft pillows

*Hold your
partner tightly,
but try not to
place all your
weight on her*

LAP SITTING

*In this position, lower yourself
onto your partner when he is
seated, and use your arms to
support yourself.*

*Raise your buttocks
provocatively with your
legs spread wide to
present an exciting view*

THE DRAGON TURNS

*This position allows the
maximum possible
penetration, so
always go gently
to avoid
discomfort.*

TAO POSITIONS

THE TAOIST BOOK *T'ung Hsüan Tzu* describes 26 positions for lovemaking. As the Taoists regarded lovemaking as an art form, nearly all the positions were designed to be esthetically pleasing. Many of the techniques involve unusual juxtapositions of limbs and bodies but are deeply visually satisfying.

Support your partner's legs

TWO FISHES
Like a pair of spawning fish bending their tails around each other, the lovers lie side by side. After penetration, he lifts her legs onto his.

TAO POSITIONS (CONTINUED)

MANDARIN DUCKS

Its name inspired by the mating of mandarin ducks, this side-by-side, rear-entry position allows the man to thrust freely. There is something sly and seductive about slipping into your partner from the rear, especially if she has not been expecting it. For example, if she is asleep, it may be a surprising and erotic way to wake her.

Stimulate your breasts and nipples as he thrusts

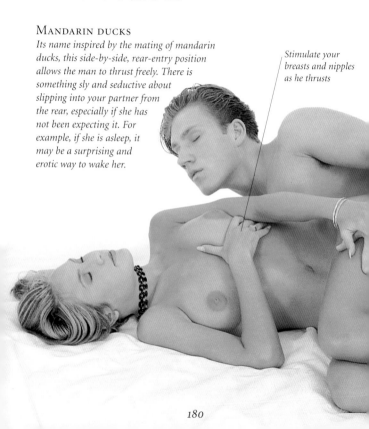

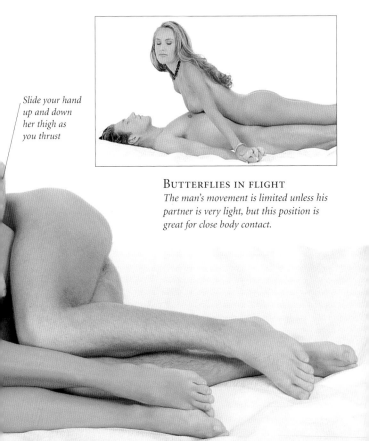

Slide your hand up and down her thigh as you thrust

BUTTERFLIES IN FLIGHT
The man's movement is limited unless his partner is very light, but this position is great for close body contact.

TAO POSITIONS (CONTINUED)

SEAGULLS ON THE WING
In most man-on-top positions, the penis thrusts downward in the vagina, but here, the penis and vagina are parallel, so that the interior of the vagina is stimulated very differently.

THE PINE TREE
This position is ideal if your penis is short because it provides deep penetration, and your partner can pull herself up and down with her legs.

THE GALLOPING HORSE

*Like a bareback rider
clinging to the mane and
tail of a speeding horse,
thrust while holding onto
your partner's neck and foot.*

*Pull him in as close
to you as possible*

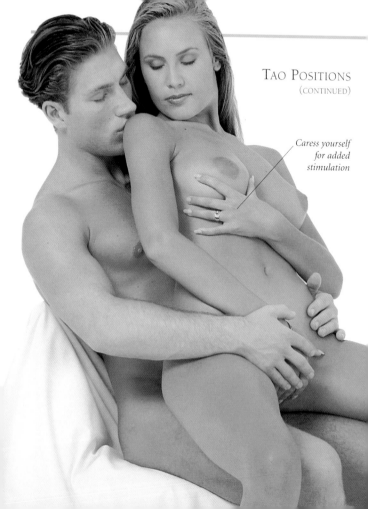

Caress yourself for added stimulation

A PHOENIX PLAYING IN A RED CAVE
The vivid imagery of this posture's name hints at the deep penetration that it allows.

Spread your legs wide for easier access

THE GOAT AND THE TREE
Although the man's movements are restricted, his hands are free to fondle his partner's face and breasts and stimulate her clitoris. This last possibility can prove vital because the woman is otherwise unlikely to reach orgasm.

EXOTIC TECHNIQUES

MOST OF THE LOVEMAKING POSITIONS in this section are inspired by a manual called *The Perfumed Garden.* This originated in male-dominated North Africa in the 15th century, and its primary aim was to instruct men on how they could enhance *their* sexual pleasure. However, many of the very exotic techniques do in fact deepen the lovemaking experience for both partners. Introducing some of these positions into your lovemaking will help to enhance your overall sexual experience.

INSPIRING AFFECTION
The Perfumed Garden *stresses the importance of inspiring affection in the woman, but these days that should be the first objective of any lover, regardless of their sex.*

VINE INTERTWINED
Prolonged intercourse is facilitated if the couple lie on their sides. She lies with one leg between his.

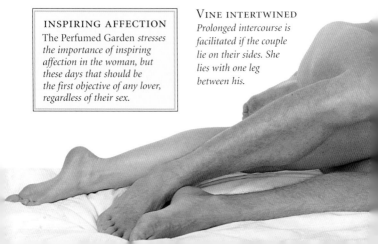

THE FIRST POSTURE

*In this position, a man with
a long penis can adjust his
length of thrust to avoid
causing his partner
any discomfort.*

*Caress your partner
slowly and leisurely*

EXOTIC TECHNIQUES
(CONTINUED)

THE ONE WHO STOPS AT HOME
Lying on her back, the woman tenses and raises her buttocks and lifts and swivels her hips as she thrusts upward. Her partner follows her movements, making sure he doesn't slip out.

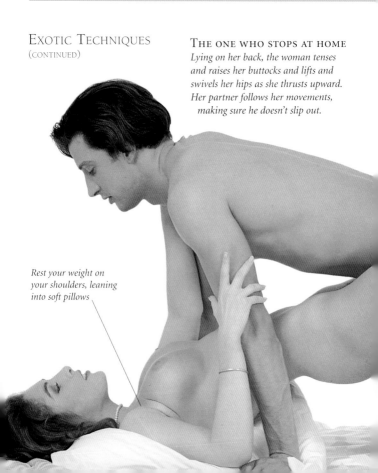

Rest your weight on your shoulders, leaning into soft pillows

FROG FASHION

*This position is quite
different. Neither
partner can move
very much, but it's
curiously secure,
cosy, and intimate.*

*Tense your
buttocks and the
backs of your
thighs as you
thrust upward*

COMPATIBILITY

*The more time you spend
making love with your
partner and trying out
different positions, the more
sexually compatible you
will become. This, in turn,
will lead to greater self
awareness and fulfillment.*

EXOTIC TECHNIQUES (CONTINUED)

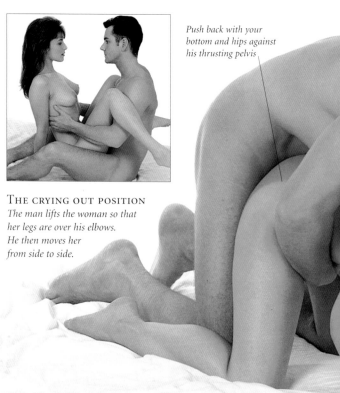

Push back with your bottom and hips against his thrusting pelvis

THE CRYING OUT POSITION

The man lifts the woman so that her legs are over his elbows. He then moves her from side to side.

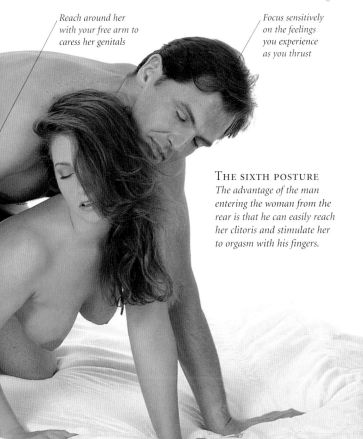

Reach around her with your free arm to caress her genitals

Focus sensitively on the feelings you experience as you thrust

THE SIXTH POSTURE

The advantage of the man entering the woman from the rear is that he can easily reach her clitoris and stimulate her to orgasm with his fingers.

EXOTIC TECHNIQUES (CONTINUED)

THE TENTH POSTURE

The woman is actually dominant in this position. She initiates movement and he responds to her rhythm.

PROLONGING THE PLEASURE

The versatile missionary position is augmented by the man pulling his testicles downward. This controls impending orgasm and prolongs intercourse.

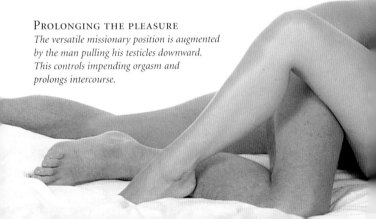

THE MOVEMENTS OF LOVE

All the positions so carefully detailed in
The Perfumed Garden *are based on eleven
different penetrational movements designed
to introduce as much variety as possible.*

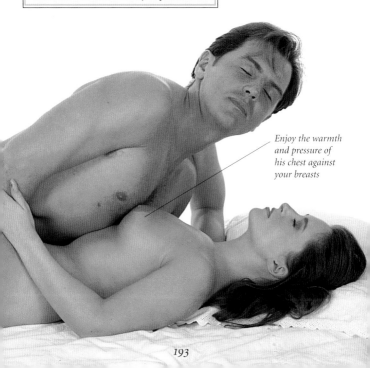

*Enjoy the warmth
and pressure of
his chest against
your breasts*

STIMULATION FOR HIM

D URING LOVEMAKING, a woman can greatly enhance her partner's sensations by using her hands and fingers to provide additional stimulation. To do this, draw on the information you have already acquired from sessions of mutual pleasuring by hand.

MASTURBATION DURING LOVEMAKING

You will be more constrained than usual, as penetration prevents a full grip on your partner's penis. But if you know a certain touch drives him crazy, do your best to incorporate it during lovemaking.

TWICE THE PLEASURE
When you are astride your partner and with your back to him, it is very easy to reach the base of his penis to squeeze it as he thrusts.

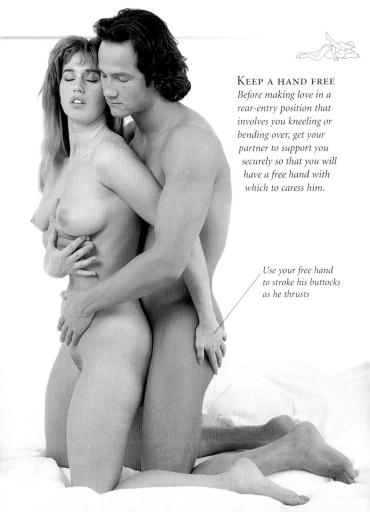

KEEP A HAND FREE

Before making love in a rear-entry position that involves you kneeling or bending over, get your partner to support you securely so that you will have a free hand with which to caress him.

Use your free hand to stroke his buttocks as he thrusts

COITAL STIMULATION

Good sex can become really great sex when you enhance the basic action of intercourse with sensual hand massage and stimulation. There are several versatile positions that facilitate hand-to-genital contact, and of course there are other areas of the body which can be reached and will respond to touch during lovemaking.

KNEELING POSITION

When your partner is on top, but kneeling rather than lying on you, it is easy to reach and massage his penis.

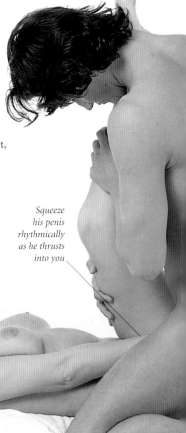

Squeeze his penis rhythmically as he thrusts into you

VERY INTIMATE PLEASURE

When you are on top of your partner in a position such as this one, you will find it easy to lean back in order to stroke the rim of his anus with a fingertip and to stimulate his perineum.

Thrust your pelvis against both her labia and hand

STIMULATION FOR HER

FOR MANY WOMEN, SEXUAL STIMULATION isn't created by intercourse alone. Add the magic ingredient of fingers, and climax becomes a serious possibility. So ask your partner what really turns her on and, while you are caressing her, make sure that you give her pleasure by massaging her genitals in ways you know she adores. Don't leave out the rest of her body, though: massage is best when it culminates at the genitals instead of just beginning and ending there.

VARY YOUR ACTIONS
Extend your caressing and stimulation of your partner beyond her genital area – by gently stroking her belly and running your fingers up the insides of her thighs, for example.

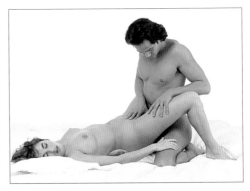

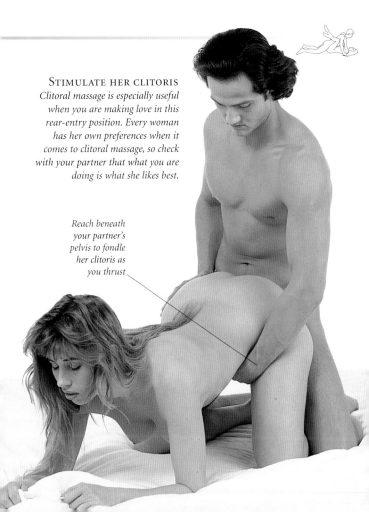

STIMULATE HER CLITORIS

Clitoral massage is especially useful when you are making love in this rear-entry position. Every woman has her own preferences when it comes to clitoral massage, so check with your partner that what you are doing is what she likes best.

Reach beneath your partner's pelvis to fondle her clitoris as you thrust

STIMULATION FOR HER (CONTINUED)

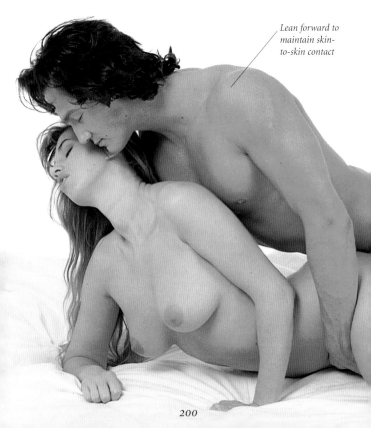

Lean forward to maintain skin-to-skin contact

KEEP YOUR HANDS FREE

In any lovemaking position where you sit upright with your partner on top of you, you will have both hands free and so will be able to caress and fondle her as you make love.

MAKE IT EROTIC

To spice things up a little in a rear-entry position, try swirling your hips around as you thrust. Doing this will give your partner a variety of new sensations as your penis rubs against the walls of her vagina.

SAFER SEX

T HE TERM "SAFE SEX" is commonly used to describe forms of sexual activity that are unlikely to expose the participants to HIV infection and thus to AIDS. Safe sex is regarded as any form of sexual activity where there is no exchange of bodily fluids – an exchange of bodily fluids being the most common way in which HIV infection is passed on.

SAFER SEX TECHNIQUES

You can reduce the risk of infection by:
◆ Using a latex condom.
◆ Stimulating each other without having penetrative sex.
◆ Having oral sex, but please be aware that this sexual activity does carry with it a low risk of infection.

IT CAN STILL BE FUN
Safe sex does not necessarily mean boring sex. You can still enjoy the experience immensely.

*Gentle caresses
can be as
loving as full
intercourse*

THE ENERGY SKIM

For most of the time, I hope you are able to enjoy a complete sexual program – from kissing to sensual massage to mutual masturbation, and then complete intercourse. But if for any reason climax is not an option, or if you have just enjoyed a massage with someone who is not your lover, you can disperse all the energy that's been generated between you by following the energy skim technique.

DISPERSING ENERGY

One of the great secrets of massage, carefully safeguarded by those master masseurs of the 1970s, is the energy skim. This technique involves massaging the energy out of the body's extremities without even touching the body. It sounds incredible, but it truly works. If anything were designed to make us believe body energy definitely exists, it's the skim. You can actually feel your body lighten as this layer of energy is removed. It can make you feel sensational.

FEEL THE ENERGY HAZE
As you hold your hands above your partner's body, you will actually feel an accumulation of energy rising up.

THE SKIM TECHNIQUE

1 Hold your hands palms down about an inch above your partner's body.

2 Imagine energy lying above his body as a haze. Make sweeping motions with both hands, and sweep that energy along the limbs and out through the body's extremities – the fingertips, toes, or head. At no point should you touch your partner.

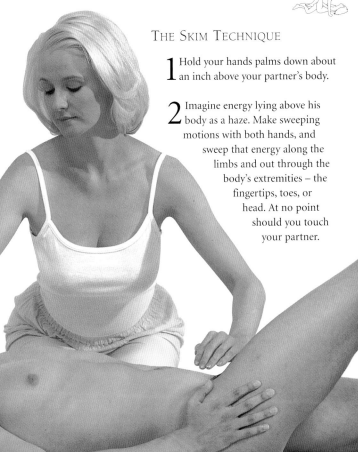

SENSUAL
MEDITATIONS

When I trained with massage master Ray Stubbs
in San Francisco in the 1970s, I was taught that for a
massage or sexual encounter to *feel* beautiful, it helped
to *think* beautiful first. Where massage was concerned,
Ray started off his sessions with a little flute music and
then talked his willing victims through a guided
meditation. If flute music is not to your taste, some
restful music (such as Pachelbel's *Canon*) on tape or
disc might be a good alternative.

PREPARING TO MEDITATE

Preparing the meditation room so that it appears welcoming is desirable. The ideal is the 1970s model where the room, with mainly white walls, is gently heated. There are green plants, and the smell of Indian incense sticks scent the air. Once you have listened to the music and begun to feel peaceful, you might take turns to read a meditation out loud.

CHOOSE YOUR MOMENT

I personally choose to meditate immediately after a massage, because the subsequent journey of the imagination feels like a poetic rounding off. But please feel free to include this treat at any stage you judge to be desirable.

A MYSTICAL JOURNEY

This meditation is the first one I ever experienced when training with Ray Stubbs in San Francisco. It consists of a journey through an alien landscape, which Ray originally brought to mind and which I have never forgotten. The purpose of a sensual meditation is to stimulate the sensual imagination. This means that the narrative does not contain many details in itself, but consists of just a bare outline. This lack of detail is designed to give you the freedom to flesh out the action with the exotica of your own mind, making the overall experience a very individual and very personal one. As with all meditations, ensure you are comfortable and relaxed before you begin.

The roaring of surf is in your ears and so is the sound of pebbles being dragged away from the beach by the tide. The sun is low in the sky and as you peer toward it, you realize that it looks older and larger and is a deep copper color.

PAUSE

Look closely now at the beach you find yourself washed up on. The rocks and pebbles are heavy with copper shadow and seem purplish underneath. The sea is warm and copper and you wonder what is in its depths.

PAUSE

Somehow you stagger from the surf and collapse onto the sands. Where have you come from? And what is there to go onto now?

PAUSE

You are seized by an overwhelming compulsion to sleep, exhausted by your battle with the water. Crawling farther from the water, you find a soft sand dune warmed by the alien sun. You curl up into its side and slip into sleep. Just settle into the sand and let your body relax.

PAUSE

And as you sleep you dream.

PAUSE

In your dream, an alien creature comes crawling
along the surf line looking for something.

PAUSE

It's looking for you. It crawls toward you and stops where
you are dozing. It's like nothing you've seen before and
yet, you can sense that it's intelligent. This is no animal,
it's a thinking being. You feel no fear. Instead there's a
warm instinct to make contact. Tentatively you touch it.
What does it feel like? What impression do you gain?

PAUSE

The creature, in turn, touches your face. In fact it
presses something onto your face. And then more
of these strange artifacts onto many other parts of
your body. Soon you are covered with these little
pressure points. Then the creature steps away from
you and waves a square stone in your direction.
Every pressure point tingles.

PAUSE

Look down at your body. What do you see?

PAUSE

As you gaze you realize that something is growing from each pressure point, binding you skillfully and closely. Frightened, you struggle to escape. And then you wake up. And you see that the dream is reality. You are cocooned in a web of light silky material and you are unable to move.

PAUSE

As you panic, a soothing voice speaks to you, inside your head, immediately calming and reassuring you. Fear not, it says, I mean you no harm. I care for you. And miraculously your head clears and your whole body feels light. Looking down, you see you are flying.

PAUSE

You fly across the alien landscape. The colors are so different from your home, the textures unfamiliar and yet this land feels warm and comforting. Take a look at this wonderful landscape. What do you see?

PAUSE

Your body settles in a cloud. It feels like cotton wool.
As you nestle in the heavens, the pressure point on your
forehead sends a sense of perfect beauty through your
brain. You have never felt so still and so pure. You feel like
spreading out wings and flying over the entire new world.

PAUSE

As you lie in your cotton cloud, the silky cocoon falls away
from your body revealing it naked, and perfect underneath.
You possess the beauty you've always wished for.

PAUSE

As you revel in such beauty the cloud next to you
begins to roll around. And, as it does so, the shape
of a beautiful lover is revealed, lying next to you.
This is the lover you have always longed for.

PAUSE

Nothing this lover does or says will harm or upset
you, ever. You know you can trust this lover deeply.
A great sense of homecoming bathes you. You are
bathed in the belief that you have come home.

PAUSE

Taking your hand, your lover walks with you toward a twisting spout of flame. It's the flame of eternal life. You see all the colors of its light spreading out before you.

PAUSE

The white of pure energy seeps into every pore of your body. You feel yourself melt apart, then re-assemble. You are clean, shining, translucent with sensuality. It would only take one feather-light touch to reach the highest level of ecstasy.

PAUSE

Streaming with that ecstasy, you pour as a shaft of white light, back into the surf that you recently came from. Only now the surf changes color. As you enter it, the whiteness from your being sends out crystal purity and the sea stretches sparkling and clear for thousands of miles around the planet.

PAUSE

You are complete. Now let the purity of the sea before you fill you and wash you and endlessly renew you. You are pure and white and at perfect gleaming peace.

ENDS

JOURNEY IN THE INTERIOR

Sensuality is about much more than sex. Sensuality comes from touching textures, hearing harmonious sounds, seeing voluptuous colors, and feeling imbued with beauty. This meditation is not specifically sexual, but I hope it will stimulate your sexual imagination. The imagination is a powerful tool. It allows you to re-experience past events or to go forward in time. It allows you to become part of a fantasy and gives flavor to the mood. Here is a meditation about journeying that I hope leaves you remembering what it was like in heaven. It returns you to your earliest experience of sensuality – a time of pre-consciousness.

Your eyes are closed. You are warm, and snug, curled up and cosy. You are safe and contained, with familiar sounds regularly soothing in your ears. You are squeezed and contained and to test your freedom you put out an arm and press it against the outside of your world where it wraps around you. You feel that world, exploring it with your fingertips and with the palm of your hand.

PAUSE

Open your eyes. A faint redness gleams somewhere below you. There's little to see. But there's plenty to touch. You run a hand across the rim of your world again. It's soft and elastic and it gives a little. Suddenly, pressure from the outside pushes back onto your exploring hand. Contact!

PAUSE

You push in return. Suddenly there are sounds. They bear no resemblance to the harmony of the deep, the deep that you have bathed in for so long. You shrink back, surprised by the noise of the outside world.

PAUSE

And yet the sounds take on a pattern of their own, a beat, a kind of rhythm. And you are moving, swaying, the liquid swishing through your limbs and back again. The fluid pours around your body, stroking and ruffling your skin, till the strokes feel as though they are inside your very being.

PAUSE

Your limbs feel at one with the tide. All of you is streaming, like seaweed with the sea flowing through it. The tide passes and re-passes. The down on your body streams with the current, while you breathe in with the ebb and flow of the water, feeling like the ocean itself.

PAUSE

The rhythm continues. It's a pressure, a forceful squeeze. It presses you hard against the wall of your world and yet it's also pleasurable. It's good to be squeezed – your skin ripples; there are prickling sensations across your chest and between your legs. You lift your arms and the prickles of pleasure come again. A wave of harmony and sensuality floats around you. Pleasure is jetted into your limpid world and now it froths and bubbles around your body and your face. You breathe in the sharpness of its sensuality.

PAUSE

You are part of this wave of pleasure. What courses through the water, courses through you, too. And the liquid streaming around your limbs quickens its pace, rubbing all your tiny pores, backward and forward, backward and forward, until you think you will disintegrate with the delight.

PAUSE

A great waft of satisfaction clouds the sea around you and bathes your face. You breathe in the endorphins and open your mouth in wonder, high on this wonder drug, which is puffed throughout your world, seeping inside your very being.

PAUSE

Suddenly you are squeezed, hard. It hurts. It hurts again. And yet the cloud of pleasure that is also you, feels the pain as another extreme. It's sensuality of a different sort – the other side of sensuality. The hurt that is pain that is pleasure, becomes an integral part of the whole of you. How, after all, could you know pleasure without some pain?

PAUSE

Inside your world, the walls are rippling in on themselves. They threaten to tear you up, to knock you flying. And yet, like a tiny cork on a great ocean, you remain bobbing along. You're a survivor.

PAUSE

And as you wonder if you should feel fear, a further current of sheer ecstasy rushes across your skin and what with the tumult of the waters, and the pain from the outside and the pleasure from within, you fall quite limp with the chaos of it all.

PAUSE

You let yourself go. Buffeted from this side to that, stretched and wrapped, squeezed and slackened – your world resembles a storm at sea. And yet you continue to bob. And bob. And bob.

PAUSE

Until the storm abates. The waters settle. The pressures cease. And there you are. Cool in the calming of the storm. You can ride out anything. And as you dream along, there is a singing in your head – a singing that comes from the poetry of voices outside your being. A poetry that repeats, many times, the words, I love you, I love you, I love you.

PAUSE

Love inside you is good. Love is an adventure. Love means action and seduction and clouds of pleasure. Love is also pain, but such seductive pain. And love is survival – there you are and there's the sea and there, throughout everything, is the steady rhythm of a heartbeat. And you think to yourself, this can go on forever. And it does go on. It continues within you, and it also persists inside your child's dreams, and in the minds of your brothers and sisters, and it rests deep inside the consciousness of friends. The sea, the journey across, the storm, and the survival are the earliest portions of human sensual experience, shaping us for the world to come.

ENDS

THE MEADOW

To carry out the following meditation you need to lie flat on your back on a comfortable surface with your eyes closed. Although at certain points during this experience you are given an instruction to close your eyes, this is only done *within* the meditation. In actuality, your eyes need to remain closed until the very end.

Sensuality has many different facets. Beauty and eroticism are strong ingredients, but so too are the emotions that are often valued less. These might be familiarity, security, the comfort of continuity, the sense that there is someone waiting for you in the background. In this very beautiful and sensual meditation, nostalgia is related to strong visual and olfactory signals.

Underneath your body is a springy surface of sedge and grasses. In your ears there's the sound of insects buzzing. A warm current of air stirs the little hairs on your skin and far off you hear the chirrup and call of small birds. As you move your hands, palms upon the ground, you discover they are resting on small, soft tufts of grass.

PAUSE

Stroke the grasses. Run your fingers through them. Feel the thin blades slip in velvet ribbons across your hands.

PAUSE

In your imagination (but not in reality) open your eyes. Around you there are tall waving fronds of meadow plants, blowing in the breeze that wafts across your face.

PAUSE

In the corner of your eye you see a scarlet flower, then another, then several dotted in the grasses surrounding you. Just beyond your right foot is a small blue cornflower; to your left, yellow and white daisies.

PAUSE

The breeze wafts again. It grows stronger. And stronger. Feel it against your skin. The moist air streams through the meadow and all the flowers and grasses sweep toward you in a concerted wave, a giant ripple that moves from one side of the meadow to the other.

PAUSE

As it travels, it enfolds you along with the rest of the flowers. Your hair streams away from you, your limbs become weightless and off you go. Your body whips through the grasses, with the fronds and flowers softly beating your skin as you traverse the field.

PAUSE

As you fly, the multi-colored flowers stripe your skin with pollen and soon you are decorated with blue and red and yellow, white and green in a striped and patchwork pattern. You blend with the meadow, you are the meadow and yet still you travel, darting at insect level through the long stalks and leaves.

PAUSE

Look to the left. There's a rabbit, lifted by the same zephyr, its button nose quivering, its short fur parted by the rush of the journey. For a time the two of you keep pace. Reach out your hand and stroke its back. It turns toward you in mute delight before being whipped away to become a black speck. You carry on with your airborne journey, streaming through the meadow, which now grows so wide it seems like a prairie.

PAUSE

The breeze is dwindling. Slowly, softly it deposits you on the bank of a small stream. Lean over the side and look into the water.

PAUSE

Can you see the fish? Can you catch the movement of their fins as they hover in the shade, keeping abreast of the current?

PAUSE

On the far bank, black and white cows graze. Listen. Can you hear the chomping of their jaws as they munch mouthful after mouthful of rich pasture?

PAUSE

The sun blazes pleasantly on your back. Sit on the
river bank and dangle your feet in the water.
Relax and savor the moment.

PAUSE

Close your eyes again and listen very carefully.
Can you hear the water? There are trickling sounds
close by, but the stream itself swirls and eddies. And
far off, almost beyond your hearing range, is that the
muffled roar of a weir? There is a disturbance in the air
and when you open your eyes you catch sight of a small
blue bird darting into a hole on the opposite side
of the stream. Hold your breath and wait.

PAUSE

The bird re-emerges from the hole and darts into the
stream right in front of the bank, where you are sitting.
Looking down, you can see the little thing; it is now
swimming underwater. It catches a minnow in its beak,
flits out again and back to its nest in the river bank.
Can you see the colors in its plumage? Can you see
the greens and blues? The iridescent sheen?

PAUSE

As you laze in the sun, lulled by the sound of the ever-running water, almost dozing, with your feet in the water, you hear someone calling you far off. "Coo-ee. Where are you? Are you there?" You recognize the voice. It is someone you love – someone who makes you feel safe. And happy. Who is it? Can you picture this person?

PAUSE

You are being called home for tea. Unhurriedly, you walk back across the meadow, following the inviting voice. Your feet pace through the long grasses and wild flowers until you come upon a cloud of small blue butterflies flickering above a clump of purple blossom. Stop and look closely at the delicacy of their movements. Can you see the batting of their wings, the intricate dance as the butterflies weave in and out of each other's flight?

PAUSE

Halt one of the butterflies in your mind's eye. Freeze it in mid-flutter so that you can look at the brilliance of its color. What kind of blue is this creature? Does the hue remain constant? Or does the blue change? Does it transmute from dark to light? Are the wings lustrous and gleaming? Or the pale, flat blue of storybooks? This is *your* butterfly. You can make it any shade of azure you desire.

PAUSE

Then release it. Let it flap back to its fellow fritillaries. As you follow the butterflies' dance again, you hear the cry in the distance, "Coo-ee. Where are you?" You set off once more.

PAUSE

The meadow slopes and you find yourself hurrying downhill. Here, the grass is brilliant emerald green, cropped by rabbits, ridged and terraced by their tiny pathways. In the distance, at the foot of the hill, in a small valley is a house. At the doorway stands a tiny figure, waving.

PAUSE

What does the house look like? It's the sole dwelling in the valley. For miles around there are only trees and fields and farm buildings. But on the

edge of the horizon if you look hard you can
see some spiralling puffs of white smoke
where a village lies.

PAUSE

As you leap down the hill in skips and jumps
the house becomes clearer as you get closer.
Whose house is it? You know you are welcome
there. You know you are expected. Seeing you
approach, the figure at the doorway goes inside.
Cooking smells mingle with the country scents.
Suddenly hungry, you anticipate the meal
you are racing toward.

PAUSE

As you enter the house the sun is going down
behind you. It's the end of the day and candles
light the room. The smell of hot baking suffuses the
evening air. At the range, in the dark, at the back
of the room, a smiling figure turns toward you,
carrying a hot plate heaped high and offers it to
you. You've come home.

ENDS

THE TREE OF LIFE

This final meditation is based on a drawing called *The Tree of Life*. In the diagram, which is also a puzzle, there are many little figures. These are perched on the tree or underneath the tree on the ground. At certain points in the meditation you will be asked to make choices about climbing the tree. The purpose of the puzzle is to decide where on the tree you might feel happiest, and then to deliberate on the reasons for your choice. After you have completed this meditation and "climbed your tree," spend some time thinking about how it made you feel and ask yourself where in the tree you felt best.

There is a picture in front of you. A pen outline of a huge spreading tree. At the foot of the tree, halfway up the trunk, and out on the limbs are people. Little men and women who dance and sing, struggle and sob, climb and fall. The tree is full of them. They are everywhere. There isn't a part of the great growing edifice that hasn't been colonized. Even the topmost branches, swaying in the breeze, flimsy and liable to break any minute, contain someone gazing upward, wondering how much farther they may safely go.

PAUSE

As you look longer, the people on the tree begin to stir. Some are climbing, two, sitting side by side on a branch, kiss, while another, in the center fork, is waving at you.

PAUSE

Now you can hear the creak of the branches and the rustle of the leaves and the chatter of the men and women perched like starlings. The person who is waving calls.

PAUSE

"Come on up," the person yells. A little surpised, you look around. And find you are standing in the picture. In front of the great spreading trunk. It is you being

summoned. You take a closer look at the caller
who seems friendly enough.

PAUSE

"It's easy to climb," they call. "Don't be afraid."

PAUSE

You take a closer look at the foot of the trunk. There is
actually someone there already, making a rather poor
job of getting up the first section. They are struggling
ineffectually, with one foot still on the ground. You
feel sure you can do better if only you can mount that
first part. The trunk is rough and although there are
no branches at the beginning of the climb you feel that
if only you can get a toehold, you could at least
make it to the first big branch.

PAUSE

"Don't do it," says a voice from behind and looking
around you see a figure getting up from a fall,
grasping their shoulder in pain. "It's impossible.
I've hurt myself."

PAUSE

You hesitate. You don't want to hurt yourself. The top of the tree does look inviting. And besides, the person calling looks attractive. If they can get up there, surely you can too. Two others are lying on the grass at the foot of the tree. "It's really comfortable here," they point out. "Wonderfully cool in the shade." As you look around you realize that it's a blazingly hot day and the tree is providing shelter from the sun's rays. It's quite tempting to flop down besides these others and laze alongside them instead of getting yourself hot and bothered with the strain of climbing.

PAUSE

But, as you hesitate, the voice calls again. "It's great here. Come on up." And you can see that the caller is standing on the middle fork, riding the tree, like a sailor in the rigging of a great ship. High in the spread of branches there's a breeze. You can see it up there ruffling the leaves.

PAUSE

So you decide to give it a go. Before you begin, though, you look hard at the person calling. Are they male or female? Are they black, white, or Asian? Tall or short? Big boned or or small limbed? What color is their hair? Is it straight or curly? What style of clothing do they wear? What is it about this person that makes him or her attractive? What is the expression on their face?

PAUSE

Now that you have visualized this new friend, you begin the upward route. The person sprawled across the first branch helps heave you that first most difficult stretch. There's a nasty minute when you think you are about to fall but you manage to regain your balance and soon you are standing and looking up at the branches beyond.

PAUSE

Already there's a view from here. As you look away, what can you see? What kind of countryside stretches out in front? It feels good to be up with the others. So good in fact that you are very tempted to halt, right where you are. But would it matter if you didn't go higher. You certainly don't have to climb any farther. You can choose to stay here at the first branch if you want.

PAUSE

IF YOU CHOOSE TO STAY HERE, READ THE NEXT PARAGRAPH THEN END. BUT IF YOU DECIDE TO CONTINUE CLIMBING, SKIP THE NEXT PARAGRAPH AND READ TO THE END OF THE MEDITATION.

You feel safe here. You have done the hardest bit and that is what feels important. You strike up a conversation with the person at the foot of the tree and when you eventually descend, they are waiting to help you down. It's a pity perhaps that you didn't get to meet the caller. But you know you have done something courageous. And you gamble on the chance that the caller will be there next time.

But you don't feel as if you've gone quite far enough. When you look up you can see the others swaying high above. Down here the tree is still so solid that there's no movement. And anyway, you want to go up to the person.

PAUSE

So you limber on. It's much easier now. Of course you have to be careful, but provided you hang on tightly, you are safe. You overtake others who have ended their own climb and are sitting or standing on the branches gazing across the horizon.

PAUSE

You are not far now from the fork in the trunk where your new friend is waiting. As you approach, they wrap their right arm around the trunk and help haul you the last stretch. They give you a welcoming hug. It feels good.

PAUSE

For a while you enjoy the view and the sense of companionship. But after a while you become aware that there is yet a higher section. You can't resist finishing the climb. You know the day will feel unfinished if you don't go as far as you possibly can and you feel pretty certain you are able to manage several more levels. Picking the branches very carefully and testing the limbs as they get smaller, you climb on.

PAUSE

The feeling at the top is exhilarating. The wind races through your hair and streams past your face. It's silent up there, the chatter of the others remains at the other levels. The view stretches out across mile after mile of unbroken countryside until in the far distance you can see the roofs of a great city.

PAUSE

Sighing with contentment you turn to come down again. And lose your footing. You start to fall. To begin with you are falling in slow motion, but as you tumble toward the ground the fall speeds up. Any second you must crash? What can you do? Can you be saved?

PAUSE

Well yes, you can. At the last minute you spread out your arms and fly. You zoom up from the ground like a small rocket and the next thing you know, you are circling the tree. You are perfectly safe. You can go anywhere on the tree and know you will be secure. So the final choice of what to do and where to go is yours.

PAUSE

Will you fly back to the new friend? Go up to the top again? Try out some of the other branches? Meet with some of the other people? Your final choice will tell you something about your own character. But the choice is yours alone. Spend as long as you like thinking about it. You can always fly back to the tree on another occasion.

ENDS

INDEX